Praise for
CEO ROAD RULES

"Solid, practical, and effective, *CEO Road Rules* cuts to the core of essential fundamentals as well as the more complex issues that arise as you climb the ladder of success."

—Michael A. Granuzzo, founder & CEO, CADDIEMASTER, INC.

"A powerful, commonsense guidepost. From focus to resiliency, *CEO Road Rules* offers the needed blend of insights and tips to inspire one to greater achievement, fulfillment, and meaningful legacy."

—Marv Tuttle, Executive Director and CEO, Financial Planning Association

"A pragmatic road map for success. Key and Stearns provide a compelling approach for improving organizational performance and personal fulfillment. A nice addition to the leadership literature."

—James C. Renick, Senior Vice President, Programs and Research, American Council on Education

"Transports you to places few other business parables can. The authors provide a simple yet powerful framework for lasting success and—perhaps even more important—significance."

"The focus on significance is key. Should be required reading for all CEOs or anyone who aspires to the role. The interviews and real-life stories bring the lessons home."

"Gives the reader a chance to rethink the basic premise of the exceedingly busy life and come to terms with the profound counter-challenges the CEO faces. It's an opportunity to pull even more victory out of the jaws of victory."

"Removes much of the mystique about what's necessary and essential for effective leadership of senior talent. Great stories and well-presented lessons."

CEO
ROAD
RULES

CEO ROAD RULES

RIGHT FOCUS

•

RIGHT PEOPLE

•

RIGHT EXECUTION

Mary Key, Ph.D.
Dennis Stearns

MOUNTAIN VIEW, CALIFORNIA

To all those who lead, mentor, and inspire

Published by Davies-Black Publishing, a division of CPP, Inc., 1055 Joaquin Road, 2nd Floor, Mountain View, CA 94043; 800-624-1765.

Special discounts on bulk quantities of Davies-Black books are available to corporations, professional associations, and other organizations. For details, contact the Director of Marketing and Sales at Davies-Black Publishing: 650-691-9123; fax 650-623-9271.

Visit the Davies-Black Publishing Web site at www.daviesblack.com.

10 09 08 07 06   10 9 8 7 6 5 4 3 2 1

Printed in the United States of America

Library of Congress Cataloging-in-Publication Data
Hessler-Key, Mary.
CEO road rules : right focus, right people, right execution / Mary Key and Dennis Stearns.—1st ed.
    p. cm.
Includes bibliographical references and index.
ISBN-13: 978-0-89106-217-2 (hardcover)
ISBN-10: 0-89106-217-3 (hardcover)
1. Executive ability. 2. Chief executive officers. 3. Executives—Conduct of life. 4. Success. I. Stearns, Dennis. II. Title.
HD38.2. H4775 2006
658.4′2—dc22

                                                                2006023693

FIRST EDITION
First printing 2006

CONTENTS

Foreword   ix

Preface   xv

Acknowledgments   xxiii

About the Authors   xxvii

1 The CEO's Ride   1

PART   ONE

FOCUS

2 The Right Road   43

3 The Right Focus   49

4 The Right Planning   69

P A R T   T W O

PEOPLE

5 The Right People   97

6 The Right Resiliency   123

P A R T   T H R E E

EXECUTION

7 The Right Execution   149

8 The Right Legacy   171

Epilogue   189

References   195

Index   197

FOREWORD

I believe there are five fundamental qualities that make every team great: clear goals, good communication, trust in each other, collective responsibility, and pride in making a difference. This is true for businesses, nonprofits, community, and families. *CEO Road Rules* goes beyond many leadership and success books to also provide practical, proven ideas on how to balance work, play, and family and create meaning in your life.

For the confident, change is opportunity. I agree with esteemed business strategist Peter Drucker, who believes that we are entering a time of unparalleled change that will test the mettle of every CEO and leader in America. It will test you in your business, it will test your relationships with your spouse and your family, and it will test your resolve to help keep your community healthy and vibrant. Are you ready? *CEO Road Rules* chronicles how many of the best and brightest in this country stay balanced in their work and personal lives while creating tremendous change for the better—and prepare themselves and those around them for anything that may come their way. Resiliency is a key skill for the twenty-first-century leader to master.

Success is often measured in terms of how much you win, how much money you earn, what deal your company is able to pull off. Time after time we find people whom the media trumpets as "successful" when their lives are a wreck. Most of these men and women would trade some of the surface success and money for a kid who respects them and returns their phone calls, or for better health, or for friends who will stick with them through thick and thin and aren't their friends because they have a lot of money.

I invest one-third of my life in earning, one-third in learning, and one-third in serving. I serve on numerous boards of directors, including one for a major regional bank; run a growing university; have tremendous community involvement; and maintain an active national speaking and leadership training business. All the while, I'm striving to be a good husband to my wife and father to my children. I don't get it perfect all the time, but most of the time, it works pretty well.

CEO Road Rules has as a fundamental theme "achieving and maintaining balance," which requires some work

to get right. Achieving balance means reaching that
happy medium between minimum and maximum that
represents your optimum. The minimum is the least you
can get by with. The maximum is the most you're capable of. The optimum is the amount or degree of anything
that is most favorable toward the ends you desire.

Let me illustrate the difference between maximum
and optimum. If you're running a marathon and you go
all-out for the first mile, you may take the lead, but the
victory ultimately will go to the runner who strikes the
highest sustainable pace. If the pace is too slow, the others will pass you. If it's too fast, you'll run out of energy
before you reach the end of the race.

The objective of a marathon runner is not to lead
after the first mile, or even after the first 25 miles. It's to
finish the entire 26 miles, 385 yards at the head of the
pack. The successful runner will find his or her optimum
pace, which is the highest sustainable pace.

You need to strike that kind of balance in your personal habits and behavior. Find the happy medium between
minimum performance and the pace that leads to burn-
out. Then you'll be ready to succeed in the long run. The
entrepreneurial leaders profiled in *CEO Road Rules* have
found the happy medium, usually through trial and error.
Their stories are instructive in how to have less trial and,
hopefully, a lot less error in your work and personal lives.

CEO Road Rules offers a number of intriguing business ideas for the leaders of closely held companies. A

theme you'll find throughout the book is the concept that Jack Welch developed with great success at General Electric: the company without boundaries. By this, Welch means the removal of all barriers to the flow of information and ideas into and through your company. In some companies, information flows through the corporate structure, but only through narrow, carefully restricted channels.

Here's how Jack Welch described the kind of organization he had in mind: "In a boundaryless company, internal functions begin to blur. Engineering doesn't design a product and then 'hand it off' to manufacturing. They form a team, along with marketing and sales, finance and the rest. Customer service? It's not somebody's job. It's everybody's job. Environmental protection in the plants? It's not the concern of some manager or department. Everyone's an environmentalist."

In an age when CEOs are often reviled by the public, we also need to return to winning with virtue, where leaders are true role models in their work and family life for their employees, shareholders, and aspiring leaders. *CEO Road Rules* shows you how, through the true life stories of dozens of truly successful entrepreneurs, to win at the game of life while doing the right thing at the same time.

The authors of *CEO Road Rules* are Dr. Mary Key, a successful leadership expert, international consultant, and executive coach, and Dennis Stearns, a nationally recognized financial and business advisor who has been in the trenches for more than twenty-five years sharing the triumphs and tragedies of hundreds of business owner clients. I've known them for many years and they both have developed reputations for excellence in their respective fields. They have brought their passion for the entrepreneur's struggle to life in the pages of *CEO Road Rules*. Key and Stearns combine their perspectives and unique skills for a fast-break drill on how to go beyond success to significance. Take the life lessons in *CEO Road Rules* and make them part of your life every single day and you will ascend to an uncommon level of success and significance, living a better, more balanced life filled with richness and satisfaction.

—Nido Qubein

Nido Qubein is a successful entrepreneur who serves on the boards of numerous companies including as chairman of the Great Harvest Bread Company, with 218 stores in forty states. He serves on the executive committee and board of the ninth-largest financial institution in the United States, BB&T, and also serves as a director of La-Z-Boy Corporation. Dr. Qubein is president of High Point University, which has campuses in High Point and Winston-Salem, North Carolina. He is also chairman of the High Point Community Foundation, chairman emeritus of the National Speakers Association Foundation, trustee on the national YMCA board, and trustee of American Humanics.

PREFACE

What do you think of when you hear the word "success"? It's one of the most frequently used words in business book titles and has been the Holy Grail for generations of up-and-coming leaders, both in the United States and abroad. Success also has more baggage as a concept than just about any other word, maybe with the exceptions of "money" and "sex."

When business books use the word "success," they often mean building the largest, most profitable company and cashing in big. As a leader, you've probably read dozens of books with themes focused on the Top 25 Business Minds, Top 50 Leaders of Our Time, and leadership secrets of everyone from Intel's Andy Grove to General Electric's Jack Welch to Microsoft's Bill Gates, and even to *Star Trek*'s Jean Luc Picard. These books have touted success principles, but have any of them told you how happy the leaders are with themselves, their life, and their choices for those parts of life that lie outside the walls of the business?

Our hands-on experience is that many of these media-hyped leaders don't consider themselves successful at all after losing the respect of their children, being on their third or fourth marriage, having their health fail—or reaching the "top" only to feel dissatisfied with their accomplishments. Many then go on a quest to "find themselves," rebuild trust with their family, or reshape their company into one that is both profitable and built to last long after the CEO is gone.

You don't have to travel on that road. You can embark on a better road, maintain balance along the journey, and build a life that is integrated, successful, and has lasting significance beyond money, fame, and power.

This book highlights the personal and business journeys of primarily private company CEOs, the leaders who are responsible for virtually all the new jobs created in this country in the past ten years. Their successes and failures, heartaches and joys, are at the core of the American entrepreneurial spirit. The men and women leading our private enterprises make tough decisions every day. When competing with big public companies, racing against the upstart next door who can start up a business faster and cheaper than ever, plus trying to manage time challenges that stress even the best personal and family relationships, how do the top CEOs survive and prosper? How do they become and remain successful in all areas of life, not just in business? How do they go from success to significance in their lives?

We bring a unique perspective to the paradox of leadership effectiveness. We have witnessed both the organizational side—Mary has spent twenty years as an organizational development consultant and coach to CEOs, helping them and their organizations achieve extraordinary results while balancing the many facets of organizational success—and the personal side—Dennis has twenty-five years of experience as a personal wealth advisor to many public and private CEOs, who often have shared their deepest secrets, successes, and failures.

The majority of the CEOs we've worked with and interviewed for this book have led closely held enterprises to success. They represent the largely unsung entrepreneurial heroes overlooked by the media in favor of the smaller, but flashier, group of public company CEOs. We have included a few CEOs who have worked in both private and publicly traded companies, because the reality is that some private companies do go public.

Even though most small to mid-size public company CEOs have short tenures these days, those we have worked with and interviewed for this book provided additional texture to the discussion of what it means to live a balanced, successful life. Is it even possible to juggle all the pieces and be good, or possibly even great, in many areas? Or are you doomed to be awesome at work and mediocre or worse everywhere else?

We know from our research and interviews that you can live a great, balanced life and be an effective CEO, friend, lover, mentor, inspiration, and creative force at home, in the community, and beyond. It's not easy, and it's certainly not for everyone. Being entrepreneurial takes guts, resiliency, and agility. Being a significance-driven entrepreneur takes an extra measure of resolve and effort that has paid off handsomely for the top CEOs highlighted in our research.

Our Approach

We could have written this book using only our direct experiences with CEOs in our professional capacity over two decades of management consulting and wealth mentoring. But we decided we wanted as many experiences to draw on as possible and a rigorous approach to our research process. We interviewed more than fifty private company CEOs, plus a few public company CEOs we have known and admired.

Here are some of the questions we asked:

- As a CEO, what do/did you see as your major accomplishments?
- What are your regrets?

- Write a speech for your last day at work. What have you and your company accomplished?

- What problem or opportunity might be happening two years from now that you can start working on today?

- What do you see happening at other companies that you wish you could duplicate?

- [If retired or in transition] What problems did you face that CEOs don't face today?

- What three traits make you successful in business?

- What three traits make you successful in your family life?

- What three traits make you successful in your quest for personal fulfillment?

- What three traits make you successful in your community work?

- If you were to die tomorrow, what would you most regret having not done? What are you happy that you did?

- What risk should you have taken but didn't?

- How would you rate your overall happiness on a 1 to 10 scale? Why?

- How satisfied are you with various aspects of your life (work, marriage, family, financial)?

- If you were advising young CEOs about the path ahead in all areas of their lives, what advice would you give them?

- What are the things that have helped you and your business most?

- What have been the most fulfilling aspects of your life?
- Do you think your work will be remembered? If yes, why? If no, why not?
- How would you like to be remembered? What's your legacy?

The answers to each question often led to a deeper discussion, which developed a rich level of insight into what these CEOs think and feel. Most were incredibly honest and admitted to challenges that would have derailed many on their path to success. Their solutions to tough times sometimes had quick traction and other times took years to work. We also noticed that some of the successful CEOs were no longer satisfied with just the external measures and trappings of success. They wanted to make a difference in the lives of others, their communities, and in some cases the world.

Many of the stories you will read include the real names of the CEOs; in a few cases, particularly in examples of what hasn't worked, we have used a pseudonym. A few of our top CEOs gave permission to use their stories but asked us not to identify them. As Jim Collins puts it so well in his blockbuster book *Good to Great,* level 5 leaders, those at the top of their game over decades, shun the spotlight. Few rock star CEOs in public companies survive the test of time. Our CEO group has many confident, driven individuals, but few strived to be on the cover of *Inc.* magazine, *Fast Company,* or *Forbes* or to be interviewed on TV.

The CEO's Ride

Our journey begins with a modern version of Charles Dickens's *A Christmas Carol* that takes you on a ride with Joe, a CEO. The story line may feel all too familiar to many CEOs reading this book. In fact, the story is a composite of actual issues that many of the leaders we've worked with and interviewed have dealt with over the years.

If experience is really the best teacher, then the life lessons presented in our story and the chapters that follow could help you get back on the right road in both your business and personal lives or stay on the right road if everything in your business and personal lives is humming right now.

After Joe's story, the chapters are divided into three parts: Focus, People, and Execution. These are the three main areas in which the best CEOs and organizations build capabilities and learn to do exceptionally well. At the end of Chapters 3 through 8 are "road rules," tips for improving and enhancing how you and those you work with lead, live, and develop others. You can get additional information on our Web site, www.ceoroadrules.com, including how to order our DVD series, which provides more tools and strategies.

We hope your personal balance between life and work is closer to that of top CEOs than it is to Joe's, but even if this book represents a major wake-up call for you, remember that it was often one comment, one event, one mentor, one disaster, or sometimes just one small nudge at the right moment in their lives that helped many of the CEOs we interviewed and worked with to get the *Right Focus* with the *Right People* and the *Right Execution* working together in a synergy that created the life they had always dreamed about or maybe never imagined.

ACKNOWLEDGMENTS

We want to thank so many people from our past and present for helping us shape this book. Like so many things in life, it's the richness of many years that gets rolled up into one experience, such as writing this book. Our clients, the CEOs we interviewed, and our colleagues, mentors, families, and friends have all contributed so much. To them we say: when you read *CEO Road Rules*, please know that writing it would have been impossible without you.

The idea to write this book came from my work with two incredible coaches, Nido Qubein, who wrote the foreword for this book, and Mark Levy, author of *Accidental Genius: Revolutionizing Your Thinking Through Private Writing*. I would like to thank my clients, particularly

Angel Ruiz, president of Ericsson, NA, for our work together on Right Focus, Right People, Right Execution; Tom Wallace, CEO of RedVector, for the opportunity to work with him over the years; and so many other entrepreneurs, such as Dr. Pamela Mooney, Mark Helow, John Bruels, and Rob Hoover. In addition, I thank the members of my *Inc.* Eagles CEO groups from the past, the CEOs I currently work with through Renaissance Executive Forums, and my colleagues and friends involved with the CEO Council of Tampa Bay.

So many colleagues have supported me, including Carol Maier, Deb Esposito, Dr. Richard Gerson, Laura Capp, Dr. Joe McCann, Robert Fritz, Dianne Butler, Darlene Adams, Cathy Karlak, Kim McCall, and Walter Hardenstine. I thank them all. Special thanks also to my home support team: my loving husband Lewis Key, Jazzie, Groucho, Joan Land, Helen Warakomski, and Katy Mims.

—Dr. Mary Key

CEO Road Rules chronicles the lives of friends and clients I have worked with closely over the years. These entrepreneurs are my heroes, going bravely into the unknown, surviving and prospering after enduring so many challenges that would deter most. They have provided a hundred graduate degrees in the school of hard knocks that are so much more valuable than any formal educational training.

My support group is also a long list of visionaries and entrepreneurs. Special thanks to Dr. Nido Qubein for his mentorship and powerful lessons over the years in Intentional Congruence. To all the mentors and friends who helped me grow and learn, and supported me through the hard times, I will always be in your debt and you will always be in my heart. To the family, friends, clients, and colleagues who have gone to the great CEO roundtable in the sky, your legacy truly lives on in hundreds of your great works. You inspire me every day to live a life that matters beyond the P&L statement. PCS, keep the light on for me.

—Dennis Stearns

ABOUT THE AUTHORS

Mary Key, Ph.D.

Mary Key heads Mary Key & Associates, Inc. (MKA), a leadership development consulting firm committed for more than a decade to helping leaders and organizations move from where they are to where they want to be. MKA specializes in teaching leaders how to be more inspiring and resilient. Key is a business consultant, a popular speaker, an author, and an executive coach of corporations around the globe. Her clients have included large companies like Ericsson, Nokia, Nissan, Infiniti, Bausch & Lomb, Georgia-Pacific, Tampa Electric, Media General, Circuit City, and Baycare Health System and many entrepreneurial ones.

Key works with CEOs of fast-growing and mid-size companies where she coaches, facilitates regular executive forums, and consults with participating CEOs. She provided one-on-one consulting and meeting facilitation to CEOs and Inc. 500 winners while serving as the executive director of *Inc.* magazine's Eagles CEO program. She has also consulted in Europe, Asia, and Latin America, and has served in leadership roles at several major international consulting firms, including Development Dimensions International and Kaset, now part of AchieveGlobal. She is also past president of a medical device company.

Key received a B.S. degree from the University of Massachusetts and a Ph.D. degree from the University of Virginia. She has authored numerous articles and several books, including *The Entrepreneurial Cat: 13 Ways to Transform Your Work Life* (Berrett-Koehler) and *What Animals Teach Us: Love, Loyalty, Heroism and Other Important Lessons from Our Pets* (Random House).

Dennis Stearns

Dennis Stearns is president of Stearns Financial Services Group (www.sfsg.net), a fee-only wealth management firm based in Greensboro, North Carolina, serving clients throughout North America. Over the course of twenty-five years he has assisted hundreds of CEOs with their personal and corporate financial planning and investment management while leading professional teams that were responsible for developing multiple business scenarios and for designing and implementing business succession plans.

Stearns is a Certified Financial Planner™ practitioner and Chartered Financial Consultant. He has an undergraduate degree in finance from the University of South Florida and holds a master's degree in financial services from the American College. He has won numerous regional and national awards for excellence in financial planning. His extensive expertise includes legacy planning for high-net-worth families and venture philanthropy, building solid financial legacies that "teach heirs and nonprofits to fish, rather than giving them a fish" for generations to come.

Stearns is a frequent speaker at regional and national events for the national accounting and financial planning organizations, and has led an advanced planning case study workshop for Charles Schwab & Co. He also led multiple advanced planning workshops for the Financial Planning Association. His scenario-building experience has extended to leading teams of experts working on stock option planning, world currency crises, investment megatrend analysis, university and community growth projects, and Good-to-Great workshops for nonprofit organizations.

THE CEO'S RIDE

Leaders who have attained success may find that going from success to significance is sometimes the most difficult part of the journey because it involves becoming more selfless. Significance is about creating meaning for those around you at work, at home, in the community, and in the world. The most developed CEOs we know see themselves as part of a broader, interconnected system. They realize that for them to grow, everyone else needs the opportunity to grow too. We have observed levels of leadership; the CEO may start out being ego driven and always looking for "what's in it for me," only to transform into a more generous and growth-oriented person who becomes interested in helping others to be their personal and professional best.

Come along with us now on the ride with Joe, the CEO, who will learn—the hard way—about the importance of creating significance.

Joe slumped in his chair and rubbed his temples to ease the tightness in his head.

He'd had to fire Tony and Sam, two senior designers in his robotics department who had, long ago it seemed, helped his partner, George, and him found their company, Chiron International.

The financials for the next quarter were weak.

There was talk of unionizing.

Sharon, his wife of eighteen years, had filed for a legal separation and their son was taking it hard.

And today was the anniversary of George's death; just two years ago, he and George had been discussing how they might take the company public when cancer swiftly ate away George's life and their plans.

"I can't believe it's come to this," he muttered. "Betrayed by what used to be my best workers and Sharon, too. Now she's poisoning my son against me. Well, she'll never get away with this."

Joe's head began to pound harder, as if something were hitting him mercilessly from inside his brain. He couldn't do anything about the company stuff right now, but he could at least take care of this thing with his wife.

He jumped up, grabbed his briefcase and the keys to his car, and bolted out of the building's side door. He jerked forward as he skidded on the snowy sidewalk. "Idiots. I'll show them they can't mess with me," he swore.

Joe pulled open the door of his black Porsche 911 Carrera and landed full weight into the low seat. This was his dream car—a reward he had given himself once his business had turned an important financial corner. Sharon's laugh flashed in his mind as he remembered their first ride in it together.

Shifting gears along the winding industrial park road, Joe sped far beyond the speed limit. He didn't care; the pressure in his head seemed to let up as his speed increased. Joe's eyes focused on the blur of Christmas lights that were already on in the early dusk as he entered Peak Trails, where he and Sharon had built their home.

He remembered the first time he had brought Sharon there. They were both so excited. As they drove around the development, Sharon wondered whether they could really afford a home in Peak Trails. Joe always thought big and remembered telling her, "It's more than possible, honey. Everything we've dreamed of. It'll all be ours."

Just five short years ago, everything had seemed to be going so well. He and Sharon were building their perfect home; Collin, his son, was starting school; and Chiron was finally getting the recognition it deserved for its innovations in robotic processes and designs.

Now everything had gone straight to hell. He kept accelerating. The power of his car calmed him. He stared forward, and his mind seemed to finally shut off. Out of the corner of his left eye, Joe noticed a boy on a bike starting to cross the street. The boy looked about ten, the same age as Collin. Joe missed living with his son: eating chocolate ice cream out of the carton past bedtime, and doing math problems while watching baseball on TV.

His heart pounded as he snapped out of his thoughts and realized his car was speeding toward the boy along the slick road. He tried not to panic. He eased on his brakes to avoid sliding through the freezing slush. He got close enough to see the boy puffing as he desperately tried to pedal out of the way of the careening Porsche.

In a flashback so intense he felt transported, Joe relived a long ago trauma: he could see the large, frightened eyes of the doe frozen in the headlights of his father's car, just as they had been that frigid December day outside of Milwaukee. Joe had screamed, "No, no—*stop*, Daddy!" His father slammed into that deer, the thud of its body reverberating through their car. Blood was everywhere. Joe had nightmares for years, waking screaming as the face of the doe haunted him.

Joe swerved around the boy into the opposite lane, but he was so focused on avoiding the kid that he didn't see the approaching car until it was only a few yards away. He gasped as his stomach tightened; then he jerked the steering wheel as hard as he could back to the right, his body a still point within the spinning car. In a rush of sound, the Porsche smashed headlong into an oak tree on the far side of the road. With an odd sense of release, Joe calmly observed the sickening crush of the impact. Then everything went black.

A Partner Returned

George was dead. Joe had made the funeral arrangements himself two years ago. Yet, here George was, walking quickly across the field toward Joe as he stood outside the Porsche, calmly surveying the damage to his beloved toy and his unconscious body inside it. He could hear sirens in the distance and see people running from all directions to help, though no one seemed to notice him standing there. This didn't strike him as being nearly as odd as the sight of his old partner approaching.

George was a short, stocky man with a long nose. He had thin lips and talked fast. George grew up in Brooklyn and prided himself on how quickly he could assess any situation. "I'm from a place where you're gonna get killed if you don't get it immediately," he often reminded others. This was his rationale for cutting people off when he grew impatient with them.

Joe cocked his head. "George? George? Is that you?" he stammered.

"No, I'm Santa Claus. Who do you think it is? Geez, you're dense sometimes, Joe!" George snapped. "You alright? What the hell are you *doing,* Joe?"

Joe smiled weakly, suddenly more frightened than bewildered. "What am *I* doing? What the hell are *you* doing? You're dead. Am *I* dead? How did you get here, George?"

"I haven't got a lot of time, Joe." George growled. "So I'm gonna cut to the chase. Do you have any idea how badly you're screwing up?"

"Guess the car's ruined," Joe admitted sheepishly, nodding toward the wreck.

"Yeah, right, the car. That's just like you, Joe, always focusing on the details and missing the big picture. You know the price of everything and the value of nothing. It's starting to catch up with you, though."

Joe scoffed, "What? What the hell are you talking about? Who are you?"

George's face grew red as he pointed his finger in Joe's face. "I'm trying to help you—you don't get it. You're so wrapped up in what you *think* is right, you have no clue."

"I have no idea what you're talking about," Joe sighed, exhausted and confused.

"Look, I can't stay here and explain. That's not my role in this. I helped create some of the problems and now I'm gonna get you the help you need from others who have some good skills, the right expertise, and experience. Now this might seem a little weird, Joe, but you're gonna be visited by these spirits, these three CEOs."

"What!?"

"Just listen to me. One is gonna show you things from your past, another stuff from the present, and the last one will show you future possibilities. You gotta pay attention, Joe, to what they tell you; it could change your life. That's my hope, anyhow—that you live your life to the fullest, really do something with your life, before some crap comes along and kills you before your time. I should know all about that, right?" George smiled a little.

"I miss you, George," Joe blurted and looked down at his feet.

"Me, too, buddy," George went on. "But I'm always close by. Don't forget that. Remember though, I'm keeping tabs on what's going on, so don't blow this."

Joe looked up, but his old partner had disappeared. What was going on? Was this some kind of delusion? Did he just imagine his dead partner's return? He'd think he was dreaming if he weren't so weary and needing sleep. "I'll worry about this later," he muttered, and slid down along the tree, closing his eyes and falling into a deep sleep.

The First CEO

An elegant man in a beige cashmere topcoat laid a strong hand on Joe's shoulder and helped him up from the ground. Joe's head was swimming, and he swayed forward until the man steadied him.

"Take it easy, Joe. How are you feeling? Can I get you something?"

Joe mumbled, "Maybe some water."

The stranger pulled a bottle of water from his pocket and handed it to Joe, who took a long sip, locking on the man's eyes as he drank. Then he remembered. "Hey. How's the boy?"

"You missed him, thank goodness," said the man, who now pulled out a white handkerchief and offered it to Joe.

"I'm Robert Haynes," he smiled. "I'm here to help."

"Are you a doctor?" Joe asked.

"No, Joe, I'm a friend of George's. Like you, I'm an entrepreneur. Well, more precisely, I *was* an entrepreneur. I started the *Glendale Tribune*. I've been watching some of your struggles, and I'd like to show you a few things that might help you. How does that sound?"

Joe didn't know how to respond. He noticed, remotely interested, as a man's body was loaded into an ambulance. "Look, I don't know what's going on around here, but . . . How could you be *watching* me? What do you mean? Hey, wait a minute, how did you know my name?"

"Don't be frightened." Robert assured Joe.

"Am I dead?" Joe asked quickly.

Robert continued, "No, you're not dead. You've been given an opportunity to see a few things, things most people never get to see. This could be a second chance for you. I'm here to show you how what you've done in the past has gotten you to the point in your life where you are now. You aren't feeling very satisfied with your life, are you?"

Joe shook his head and then remembered his conversation with George.

Robert disappeared from sight and almost instantly reappeared, driving a red BMW.

"Get in, Joe. It's time to go for another ride," Robert said mysteriously.

Though he didn't relish getting in another car, Joe already needed to get off his feet and rest again. Besides, Joe felt somewhat curious about what this stranger who claimed to know George wanted to tell him.

Something about Robert made Joe feel like he was an old friend, someone from his father's generation. The way he dressed, the way he spoke, and his fatherly style all made Joe feel curious and strangely reassured.

As Robert's car sped forward, Joe was shocked to realize that they were back in Milwaukee. Robert glanced over at Joe. "Surprised to be back home?" he asked.

"Well, uh, yeah," was all Joe could say.

"I want you to visit Georgia Timberland, the old mill where you and your father worked. Do you remember going to work with him, Joe?"

"How could I forget?" Joe declared. "He worked so hard on that floor and for so little money. I always said that *I* would never work that hard for someone else. And I haven't."

Joe was proud that he hadn't compromised himself to make others rich at his expense. Once he stopped working at the mill to put himself through college, he never looked back. He got a business degree, married Sharon, and moved to Chicago to work for UT Robotics.

He did his best and, in a few years, earned the title of plant manager. He met George, and they got the idea for integrative robotics, a process that took the industry to a new level. Joe and George would often meet for lunch or after work to brainstorm about starting their own company.

Tony and Sam, design engineers at the company, would sometimes join them and help with specific design ideas. Because they were both hands-on people with a knack for figuring out how to get things to work, Tony and Sam could pinpoint design subtleties most wouldn't notice.

As the BMW pulled into the parking lot, a sandy-haired, muscular man with broad shoulders waved to a friend. Joe was amazed to see his dad again. He found himself tearing up at the sight of his young father.

"Wow," he told Robert. "I'd forgotten how he looked back then. And this place . . . my grandfather got a job here sweeping the floors, straight off the boat from Poland, and then my dad took a spot here just out of high school. It was supposed to be temporary, so baseball scouts checking out the company players would spot him and take him to the minor leagues. He dreamed about playing pro baseball for the Cubs. I guess he was really good at one time, and scouts approached him once in a while, but it just never happened for him. And he finally gave up. It's so sad."

Joe remembered that things got worse for his father as he was passed over for promotion at Georgia Timberland more than once, and he started hanging out with his friends after work, drinking whiskey at the local bar before leaving for home.

After having a few with the boys, Pete would come home late, sullen, angry, and looking for a fight. Joe learned to catch his dad early if he wanted to be with the man he had known and loved as a boy. He had missed his dad during those years.

Joe looked at Robert with tears in his eyes, "Why are we here? It's not possible that my dad is here. What does this mean?"

Robert placed his hand on Joe's shoulder again, and suddenly they were on the shop floor.

The sounds and smells and bright lights of his dad's old shop overwhelmed Joe. No one seemed to hear or see Robert and Joe, as if they had walked onto a TV show set without the characters realizing they were peering in on them.

His ears perked up at the sound of his father's calm, level voice being interrupted by someone clearly working up to a rage.

"Pete, how 'bout if you just keep your comments to yourself?" the red-faced foreman said, practically nose-to-nose with Joe's dad.

"Look, the guys have some good ideas about how to make our product better. Can't you just listen for a minute?" Pete asserted calmly.

"I don't want any crap from you. You're here to play baseball, and you think you're such hot stuff. What do you think you'll accomplish? Back off, Pete—we've got this handled. You act like a union steward or something. It's not your job to represent the guys. *I'm* the boss here. If you don't like it, leave!"

Joe's heart ached as he saw his father try to stand up for his ideas, only to be shut down. Joe cried out, "That bastard! Don't let him treat you like that, Dad."

Pete lowered his shoulders and, shaking his head, walked away.

"So, what do you think happened here?" Robert inquired, sliding his eyes toward Joe.

Joe was furious. "Are you kidding me? How dare they treat Dad this way? I can't believe he just took it."

"Do you think any of *your* employees have ever felt this way, Joe?" Robert continued.

"What do you mean?" Joe snapped.

Robert began to walk down the corridors of Georgia Timberland and turned the corner to the plant manager's office. Joe followed him in the door, ready to take Robert down a peg or two, only to find himself face-to-face with a younger version of himself.

"Oh, now this is . . . screwed up. What is going on here, Robert? Am I losing my mind?"

Robert, sitting in the corner, placed his index finger to his lips to silence Joe. Joe was stunned to see himself many years younger, sitting at his old mahogany desk on the black leather chair with the squeaky wheel. This was his office while he was at UT Robotics in Chicago!

Ellen Rock, a supervisor and a different kind of squeaky wheel, stood in front of the desk, complaining, as always, about how the employees were being treated.

"Damn it, Joe," she pleaded, her voice growing louder in her frustration. "We're going to lose some of our best workers. You've got to stop pushing so hard and taking people for granted. We keep adding bodies and asking people to work under such cramped conditions. Even though the company is doing well, we seem to cut corners with the people who make it happen."

Young Joe's eyes turned cold as he sat back, only half-listening. He stared blankly at Ellen while she ranted. "I'm not about to sit here and let her raise her voice to me. She's so emotional," he thought. "Besides, Ellen is always taking the worker's side. She's not long for management if she keeps that up."

Joe broke his silence. "Look, Ellen, calm down. There are a lot of things about this business you don't understand," he said, speaking slowly, as if she were a child. "We need to make our profit margins. And I don't have money in the budget to increase overhead right now. What *solutions* do you have? Hmmm? All I hear is your usual list of complaints and problems."

"How can you say that, Joe?" Ellen snapped back. "I've presented you with several proposals on what we can do to rearrange the floor space and on how to compensate the workers differently so they are rewarded for going the extra mile."

"That all costs money, Ellen," Joe growled.

Joe stood transfixed as he watched the younger version of himself put Ellen in her place. Robert pulled on Joe's sleeve to signal it was time to go.

As they walked out of UT Robotics into the cold, dark Chicago afternoon, neither man spoke until Robert asked, "Ready to get a cup of coffee and talk?" He placed a hand on Joe's shoulder.

Joe nodded silently, and they were suddenly in a booth at a nearly empty diner around the corner.

"What did you see as you watched yourself with Ellen in the past?" Robert asked casually.

Joe gazed into his cup. "I saw myself being very hard on her. The funny thing is, I didn't remember it that way. I guess I wrote Ellen off as a social worker type who didn't under-stand that we needed to make a profit."

"How was that scene like the one you saw your dad experiencing?" Robert pressed.

Joe raised his eyes with sudden recognition. "Wow, I *did* sound like his old supervisor, the one I wanted to hit. I wasn't as 'in your face,' but I still refused to listen. Why was I so closed off?"

"What do you think you could you have done differently?" Robert continued.

"Well, I remember really wanting to make outstanding numbers so I could show corporate what a great plant manager I was and so I could make the top of my bonus scale. I was proving myself to others, and despite the conditions Ellen talked about, we were still doing well, numbers-wise." Joe paused. "I could have given more support to Ellen and the people on the floor. Money wasn't really as tight as I used to emphasize it was. . . ." His voice trailed off.

"Do you know what happened to Ellen?" Robert asked.

"Uh, no," Joe answered, embarrassed to realize he'd never thought of her since he left UT Robotics.

"Well, you might remember passing her over for the manager of operations spot, even though she was considered the most capable. The employees really wanted her to get the position, too, because they felt she was fair and listened to their concerns and ideas. And because you felt like she burned a bridge with you, your comments to others—supposedly off-the-record and in her personnel folder—followed her for the rest of her career. She lost her motivation and eventually was let go during the 'rightsizing' that occurred after you left. Like your dad, Ellen let her dreams die because she couldn't find a way to make them grow. She now works as an assembler in a nearby plant and struggles with depression."

Joe winced as he realized the impact his actions had had on someone else's life.

Robert paused and watched Joe for a moment as he looked down. "There is another way, Joe. At my old company, the *Glendale Tribune,* we were able to engage the minds and hearts of our employees and managers while growing profitably. We did this through what I call Right Focus. Would you like to hear more?"

Joe nodded.

"First, Joe, I'd like to ask you a few questions."

"Sure, fire away," Joe agreed. "I seem to have nothing but time at this point."

"Alright," Robert continued. "What was your vision for the company you started with George?"

"Well, we saw our company as *the* innovator in the robotics industry, and we wanted to grow exponentially. We used to say '$500 million in 5 years' like a mantra to each other and to the employees," Joe smiled proudly.

"What kind of a reaction did you get from the employees when you'd share your vision?" Robert prodded.

"Honestly, it was mixed. We had some employees who were excited about the idea of growing, some who liked the opportunity to innovate, and others who just weren't onboard."

"What kind of environment did you have at your company when you were getting started, Joe?"

"Well, initially we had a core team—me, George, Tony, and Sam, who came from UT Robotics together. We took ideas from all the meetings and conversations we'd had and started Chiron International out of nothing. We hired about forty people the first year, and off we went. Those were exciting times. Everyone pitched in to get things off the ground. We worked long hours, but it was so exhilarating. We had ups and downs, but we were all working for the same thing . . ."

"You look a little sad," Robert responded.

"Yeah," Joe sighed. "As we got larger and took on more complicated projects, we lost that team spirit. Everyone had their own agendas, and people didn't connect with each other anymore. Like, the engineers fought with the people over in manufacturing all the time. I felt more like a referee than a CEO. But, still, we accomplished so much in spite of ourselves. I miss those old times."

Robert nodded in acknowledgment. "At the *Glendale Tribune,* we started like you did: small at first and then exploding, so there were inevitable growing pains. People were unclear about what was expected of them, we lacked teamwork, saw margins eroding. Then I discovered the importance of Right Focus."

"What do you mean, Right Focus? What's that?" Joe asked.

"Well, Right Focus is about having a dream big enough that everyone who is willing can participate in it and feel good, not only about the results they achieve, but also about how they get there."

"How they get there?"

"Right Focus is made up of four main parts: *mission, vision, values*, and a clear understanding of the *core focus* of what your organization can be best at. Mission answers the question 'What's the purpose of our company? Why are we here?'"

Joe interrupted, "Everyone knows that—to make money."

"That's where you've got it wrong, Joe," Robert said.

"You can't run a business if you don't make money," Joe argued.

"No, mission is bigger than self-interest; it's about finding the higher calling for your organization and, ultimately, can inspire a higher sense of purpose for each employee as well. Our mission reminds us whenever we get off-purpose.

"Vision answers the question 'Where do we see ourselves going?' So we took an honest look at where we wanted to be in the next five to ten years.

"Because you never had a clear vision for everyone to participate in, things got rough at Chiron. As you grew, making money and keeping the status quo seemed to be the biggest priorities," Robert said.

"I hate to admit it, but you're right," Joe agreed. "I think that's why Tony and Sam were so unhappy at the end. They kept telling me I had changed and that what excited them about our business was gone."

Robert nodded. "Good. And I've just shown you what's at stake when an organization doesn't have developed values. Your dad approached his supervisor with an innovation that

could have been a whole new business line for Georgia Timberland, but he was treated as if he was being disrespectful
toward authority by a supervisor who clearly felt threatened.
The worst thing an organization can do is stop listening to its
employees, especially those closest to the work. If innovation
were valued at your dad's company like it has been at mine,
he would have been *rewarded* for his initiative, not ignored or
chastised. Ellen, too.

"What made our company great was not just having a
vision that everyone could buy into but also having a set of
core values—like integrity or doing the right thing—that
served as our guiding principles and couldn't be compromised
for financial gain. When an organization spells out core values that everyone is expected to take seriously, everything can
change."

Joe shook his head. "I can see what you mean, Robert.
Why didn't I see this before?"

"The important thing is that you see it now," Robert
emphasized. "Next, the group asks itself what its core focus
is: 'What is this organization best in our world at?' Simply
said, Right Focus is about defining your direction: how you
treat each other and how you get there."

"And these same principles apply to your life: *you* are a
miniature organization of sorts. As I lived the Right Focus
principles, clarity set in. I became more fulfilled. I realized
that my personal purpose deals with growing things. Beyond
the pleasure of seeing our company grow, I love helping others grow in their lives. I grow in turn. That's why I'm here with
you now."

As Robert turned to get the car, he added, "I find if I can use my core strengths and complement them with those of others, true synergy happens. The team together far exceeds the sum of its parts."

Standing at the curb as Robert drove up, Joe felt light-headed and exhausted. He longed to sit back down. He got into the car slowly and reclined the seat. Within minutes, he was sound asleep.

The Second CEO

When Joe woke up, he was back at the crash site, alone. The car had been towed away, leaving muddy tire tracks and foot-prints, along with shattered glass and something Joe thought must be blood. His blood.

"I better see if I can find some help," he said, struggling to stand up and then giving up to rest for a minute. George wasn't there, nor was Robert, and it occurred to Joe that he had sustained some kind of head injury that was making him imagine all this. Robert made sense, but how could Joe have traveled to his past like that? Was this even real, now, this moment? Maybe he had been *dreaming* that he was in some kind of time warp . . .

The ringing of his cell phone in his coat pocket snapped Joe from his reverie. "That's a relief. Guess I *am* still in the real world," he thought as he flipped the phone open.

"Hello," he began. "I could use some help here. . . ."

"Hi, Joe. This is Janice Allison. I'm the CEO of All-Com Insurance. I'm calling to let you know that I'll be picking you up in a minute. George asked me to spend some time with you." The phone went dead.

Joe quickly hit "received calls," but the call information said only "private." Frustrated, Joe threw the phone down into the snow. "What next?" he yelled. Joe hated not being in control.

In a matter of seconds, Janice pulled up alongside Joe and rolled down the window. She was driving a silver Honda SUV and looked kind of like one of the soccer moms in his neighborhood on her way to pick up kids from practice.

"Hi, Joe, I'm Janice. My friends call me Jan. Get in the car."

He considered refusing, yelling at this woman that he was no fool, that this was all impossible, but he found himself settling into the warmth of the SUV, asking, "What's this you said about my partner, George?"

Jan smiled. "George mentioned that three of us would be meeting with you to help you change your present course, didn't he? Let me take you for a drive around your neighborhood. I believe there are some important things right in your backyard that you haven't been seeing."

Jan took Joe to his son's elementary school. The noise got louder as they parked by the field. "When's the last time you went to one of your son's soccer games?" Jan asked.

"Uh, I guess about a month, maybe a month and a half." Joe couldn't believe it had been that long. He had been so absorbed in the business—the downturn in the market, his shrinking margins, and rumors of unionizing kept him at work day after day, long into the night. Also, he hadn't wanted to run into Sharon.

He walked alongside Jan to the field as one of his former neighbors was passing by.

"Hello, Fred," he said, feeling obligated to acknowledge the man. Fred just walked past as if ignoring Joe.

"They can't see you, Joe," Jan stated flatly.

"This is going to be like being with Robert, then," Joe realized.

Joe saw her instantly: a pretty blond with thick layers of hair and a turned-up nose talking to another woman as they sat bundled up on the bleachers, watching their children play. Joe and Jan took the empty seats behind the two women.

Sharon looked tired but still as beautiful as she had been one May evening, fifteen years before, when Joe had asked her to dance at a university homecoming party. From that evening on, they'd really never parted.

"I'm worried about Collin," Sharon told the woman next to her between plays.

"What's wrong?" The other woman turned to look at Sharon.

"Since Joe and I split up, he seems very depressed. Look how he's playing. He doesn't have that same energy."

"Any chance you and Joe will get back together?" the woman asked.

Sharon's eyes filled with tears. "I don't think so, Carol. Things have really changed between us. I don't even recognize Joe now. He used to be interested in our life together as a family, in *us* instead of just his work, but not anymore. He used to spend all of his free time with Collin, and sometimes he'd call me up and ask me out for a date, even though we'd been married for years . . . but it's all about his business and making money now. I know he's been under more pressure since George died, so I've tried to stick it out, but I don't see any light at the end of this tunnel. So I felt I had to take the first step and file for a separation. Collin and I have to go on with our lives. . . ."

Joe sat staring at his wife, aching to hold her. He hadn't realized the pain she had been suffering. They argued so much that he saw only her angry side. Joe had been so frustrated with her; he hadn't been able to figure out what Sharon really wanted. It wasn't as if he could just leave his responsibilities at the plant to attend to their personal life. He took care of the family financially, and Sharon could have anything she wanted. He had built her a great home, she didn't have to work, and he never questioned what she spent money on.

Yet, Sharon continued to substitute teach and volunteer. She could have had a new car every year, but she still drove her old brown Toyota Camry. Holding on to her old car was her way of holding her ground, Joe often thought, in their constant battles over money. She wanted to be debt-free and to build a nest egg; he liked to take risks and leverage his assets for a greater return downstream.

Joe followed Jan to the players' bench and stood as near as he could to his son, though Collin, huddling in the cold air, didn't seem to feel his presence.

Watching his son leave the bench, Joe was surprised to see how tall Collin was getting; he hadn't noticed until now that his son had grown several inches since the last time he had really looked at him. Joe was also stunned to see that Collin didn't seem excited about the chance to make this play. He loved soccer, he was strong and agile, but now he had a merely dutiful look in his eye—like "I won't let you down," but without a spark.

Still, he moved gracefully down the muddy playing field. One of the opposing players came at him from the right side, and Collin lost control of the ball.

"Watch your side!" Joe yelled.

"It's time to go, Joe," Jan said kindly.

"I'd like to stay and watch. Collin needs me," Joe replied, trying to ignore her.

"Yes, he does, Joe, but he doesn't know you're here right now."

As the two left the soccer field, Joe tried to reassure himself and Jan. "He wasn't on today. Usually, he'd go after that chance to break the tie."

"Your family is obviously important to you, Joe. What did you notice from watching them here today?" Jan asked.

"It's hard to talk about it. I guess I didn't realize how my not being there for my wife and son has affected them," Joe replied quietly. "I'm angry with myself for letting things get out of hand. I get so absorbed in my work, especially when I see where things could always be better at Chiron. I guess I thought Sharon could handle my work schedule. After all, she has for the past fifteen years."

Joe paused, then said quietly, "Sharon's leaving really threw me. She's been through hard times with me, and I assumed she'd always be there. But I haven't really been doing anything to make her want to stay, have I? After hearing her today, I believe she still loves me. For a year now, she's begged me to go to counseling with her. But I refused."

"How come, Joe?"

"It's embarrassing to me for someone I don't know to hear our problems. It felt like a test I was going to fail. I should have tried. I can be pretty stubborn, I know, so stubborn that I haven't seen how hard our breaking up has been on everyone. Collin puts up a good front when I'm with him, but I can see now that's exactly what it is—a front."

Before he knew what was happening, Joe and Jan had parked at Chiron International and were walking toward the employee entrance of the building. Jan led the way toward the director of human resources' office. There stood Jose Garcia, speaking on the phone with someone.

"No, Joe fired them," Jose was saying. "No one knows exactly why. Joe isn't in today. Yes, I tried his cell. I've also called his wife. I couldn't get her, either. This is a real mess. We don't have the bench strength to replace Tony and Sam. Phase two of the Lockleer contract is due for completion on the tenth of this month.

"As if that's not enough, Tony and Sam's attorney called. We're going to have a big lawsuit on our hands, not only for lack of cause for firing them, but also for allegedly stealing their intellectual property."

Jose waved his hands as he spoke. On better days, he had an infectious smile and was one of those people who made you feel comfortable almost instantly. Today, he looked liked he might never smile again.

Joe collapsed into one of Jose's upholstered chairs and held his head with one hand. "How did all of this happen?" he muttered. Jan sat in the chair next to Joe.

Jose said good-bye and immediately began to speed dial someone else.

"Hello, Tom? This is Jose at Chiron." Jose now stood staring out the window. "Not so great. We've got an urgent situation here. Joe and I had discussed Tony and Sam's poor attitude of late. We agreed that we didn't have a lot of data in our files documenting our taking disciplinary action. Joe was to meet with each of them this morning to have an on-the-record discussion about why their behavior needed to change. Apparently, he met with them last night instead and wound up firing them both. He's not here, and no one can get in touch with him. I just got a call from their attorney, and . . . Can you come here right away? Thank you. I really appreciate it."

Another call came through immediately. "Jose Garcia here."

Jose stood motionless as the blood drained from his face.

"What? Where? How bad is it? When can we see him?" he asked with controlled calm. "Thanks, officer."

Jose hit the intercom button to his assistant. "Call everyone together for an emergency management meeting. Joe's been in an accident. He hit a tree near his house. That was the police. Joe's at Mercy General. In a coma."

The Meeting

As the management team convened, questions and comments flew around the room.

"No more news yet on Joe's status?"

"We were just working on some new designs the other day. Joe really knows his stuff. What a shock to hear that he's in a coma!"

"There's the Tony and Sam thing and this . . . How should we handle the press, do you think?"

"We're hurting right now. I don't know how we'll meet Lockleer's schedule. It was a real stretch *before* this accident."

Tom Trout, the head of manufacturing, leaned in to speak to Margaret Witkowski, Chiron's head of communications. "I really hope Joe pulls out of this," he whispered, shaking his head. "I knew firing Tony and Sam might have had a bad effect on him. All those guys went way back . . . Frankly, I was kind of surprised that he fired them—not that they didn't deserve it. What ungrateful complainers those guys were. I wish I could have been a fly on the wall when he did it. Joe didn't want me there. He thought it would make things worse."

As Jamie Klein, the head of sales, called the meeting to order, Jan and Joe found seats in the back of the conference room. Joe was growing more comfortable with the strange experience of being invisible and actually looked forward to watching what his staff would do without him there.

Jamie continued, "We've had challenging times in the past and made it through, and we'll make it through this, too;

but we have some critical things to attend to. We need to decide on our short-term strategy in light of Joe's accident. Let's develop an agenda together. Each of us can give an update on the status of things as we see it, and then we can address the specific items that we have added."

Each of the managers contributed their items to the agenda, and Jamie laid ground rules for good communication among them. Margaret suggested an issues list to allow discussion of non-agenda items after the agenda had been covered.

Joe turned to Jan, dumbfounded. "Wow, this is pretty impressive. I've never seen the team like this before."

"What do you mean?"

"Well, I usually get up in front of the room and go over the items on my agenda. Everyone chimes in when they want. By then the meeting's usually over, and there's not a lot of time for covering other issues."

"Watching your team today makes you proud of them, I bet."

"Definitely. They all seem to be stepping up to the plate."

"You know, Joe, you're seeing a working example of what I call the Right People principle. Right People is all about the importance of selecting the talent you need for the future as well as supporting the growth and development of the people you have in place."

"You can see by watching my team that some of them stand out as leaders, like Jamie," Joe said thoughtfully. "Others might not have been the best hires, like Tom Trout.

Tom made the situation with Sam and Tony a lot worse. He could be a real troublemaker, and he and Tony and Sam never got along. That's why I decided to handle the situation with them myself—or, I guess, *mis*handle it." Joe's face flushed as he recalled the scene in his office.

Jan sensed Joe's disappointment in himself and asked, "What could you have done differently when you were hiring for Tom's position as the director of manufacturing?"

Joe looked up as he recalled a heated discussion he had had with Jose.

"Well, Jan, Jose got problematic information from some of the people that Tom gave us for references, but I was getting impatient to hire someone. We had been advertising for this position for a while. Jose wanted to continue looking for candidates. I didn't think either Tony or Sam could do the job. The longer we looked for someone, the more irritated Tony and Sam seemed to get. I felt like we needed an experienced person to come in and help with the growth we were experiencing. Jose disagreed and let me know it. In retrospect, I see he was right.

"'You'll regret this decision Joe,' Jose said, and I still pressed forward. Tom uses a 'my way or the highway' approach with his employees. The rumblings Jose heard when he spoke to Tom's references turned out to be a much bigger issue than I had imagined."

Jan nodded. "A lot of leaders make this same mistake. When you run the company, you can use your weight and push aside other opinions, but haste winds up making more work for everyone, not to mention the backlash of picking someone who isn't a good leader for a key role.

"When All-Com's leadership team developed and implemented our Right People approach, we committed to each other that we wouldn't settle for less than the best, no matter what. If we have *any* doubts about a candidate, we keep looking. We've gotten a lot better at this over the years. We learned that we needed to improve how we found great candidates so that we have more people to pick from. We also needed to find a systematic way of screening them for the best fit.

"Even before I became CEO of All-Com," Jan continued, "I implemented three people principles throughout my career that really made a difference in selecting and developing the Right People. The first principle is *past behavior tells you volumes about future behavior.* People display certain skills and aptitudes as well as attitudes about life that stay pretty constant, unless some dramatic change occurs. I look at the skills of people, their attitude and motivation, and what others have observed about them in the workplace. What has worked for you?"

"I wish I could say that we've been that systematic," Joe commented. "Jose has helped us make some improvements, but our practice has always been to find people when we need them; sometimes that works and sometimes we make hasty decisions that backfire."

Jan nodded. "When our leadership team developed the Right People approach, we spent a lot of time thinking through the critical elements of what goes into a great hire. Which brings me to the second Right People principle—*select people with the right attitude and emotional skills.* Some call this emotional intelligence: self-awareness, assertiveness, ability to empathize, flexibility, impulse control, and optimism. These factors and others predict how effectively people will work with each other and how successful they will be in their career and in life. *Lack* of emotional skills is the biggest reason people in leadership roles fail."

"Interesting . . . wonder how I would test on *that.*" Joe commented.

"From the looks of things, Joe, I'm willing to bet that at times you haven't behaved in an emotionally intelligent way with your staff *or* your family. It was pretty obvious at the soccer game today that Sharon doesn't believe you understand how she's feeling. Could that same dynamic be playing out in the situation with Tony and Sam?" Jan asked.

Joe's body got tense. "What was I supposed to have done differently?"

"For one thing, you might have used empathy. You could have shown them that you understood what they were experiencing. That's emotionally intelligent behavior. Do you feel like you've been able to empathize with others enough to show them that you understand their world and relay that back to them?"

"What, that I *agree* with them?"

"No, Joe, that you can appreciate their feelings, views, and values, even if they are different from yours," Jan explained further.

"Guess I didn't look at it that way. Tony and Sam both accused me of not appreciating their contribution to the business and of taking advantage of them. I heard that and then I just got mad."

"So, let's try this, Joe. The first step in empathizing is to suspend judgment and ask yourself, 'If I were this person, how would I feel and why?' How do you think Tony and Sam felt, Joe, and why? Put yourself in their shoes for a minute and don't think about defending yourself."

"If I were Tony and Sam, I'd feel . . . cheated."

"Great, Joe. Go on, why?"

"They feel cheated because they gave a lot to Chiron but don't have the money, position, or respect to show for it."

"Exactly. Can you see the power of conveying that you understand that to Tony and Sam before you explain *your* view of the situation?" Jan asked. "The ability to empathize helps you find common ground with others because you are showing them that you can appreciate where they are coming from before going on to find a new solution or next step."

"There's so much I want to ask you about this, Jan. I'm thinking that I could see trying empathy with Sharon. I want her to know I understand where she's coming from, even if I don't agree with all her ideas. You've got me thinking."

"And feeling, I hope," Jan smiled. "I want to tell you about the third Right People principle because it's almost time for me to go."

Jan and Joe left the meeting room and walked down the hall to Joe's office. Joe lay down on the couch, propping his head up, and Jan sat on the chair opposite him.

Jan continued, "The third principle is *develop your successor/s*. Have you thought about your successor, Joe?"

"Not really. Until George died, I thought I'd go on forever, you know? Now I know that's an illusion. I got so busy with customers, growing the business, and other things, I never had time to formally coach anybody." Joe stared out the window, lost in his thoughts.

"At All-Com, we believe everyone needs a coach, and we set up formal and informal coaching and mentoring for our team members."

"Doesn't that cost a lot, Jan?" Joe blurted out.

"I thought it would be expensive, too, Joe. What we found was that the more emphasis we placed on helping each other be successful, the more innovation and teamwork we showed. We became more productive, and our growth has accelerated as a result."

"Yeah, but how do you find time to coach others when the wheels are about to fall off your business?" Joe demanded.

"When you are in a crisis situation, it's harder to think you have the time, Joe. But coaching isn't something that's separate from your business. Right now your management team members could use some coaching help, couldn't they? This crisis is an opportunity to be better *together.* Coaches come in all forms: other team members, outside consultants, peers, those closest to the problem, even customers."

Joe nodded and noticed that he felt as if weights had been attached to his eyelids. He thought that he would close his eyes to rest them for a minute as he continued to talk with Jan. Jan smiled as Joe began to snore.

The Third CEO

When Joe awoke, Jan was gone. Bright light pierced his eyes. He sat up and was startled to find a tall man in a gray suit staring down at him. The man smiled broadly and offered his hand to help Joe get up off the couch. "You've been sleeping for quite a while, Joe," he said, softly. "It's time to wake up. I'm Darrell Banks."

"Where am I?" Joe mumbled.

"We're at Chiron, but it's ten years after your accident. I'm here to show you the possibilities for the future. Nothing is set, but several options are emerging. The first is this." Darrell clapped his hands, and the window shade opened. The sign in front of the building read "Benfold Enterprises."

"What's Benfold Enterprises?" Joe demanded.

Darrell spoke deliberately. "It's what will happen to your business if you continue along the path you've been taking. In other words, Joe, Chiron will be out of business." Darrell nodded toward the sign. "Benfold will buy your property for its operation. In this scenario, Joe, you no longer head Chiron; in fact, the company has gone bankrupt."

"Well, that's pretty direct," Joe gulped. "What's the alternative?"

"If I had to sum it up, it's change or die. If Chiron doesn't improve how it executes, its fate is sealed. However, you do have options. I'd like to tell you about some strategies that helped me with Right Execution when we built Inmel."

"Right Execution? What's Inmel?"

"Inmel is a computer business I started with several friends from business school. Our model has been to offer twenty-four-hour turnaround using outside partners to customize, ship, and offer services to our customers. We make it simple for our customers to get what they need and get online within an hour of set-up. Our business launched an array of advanced technologies, such as the ability to use all five senses while interacting with others online."

"No way. This *must* be a dream." Joe looked pale as he tried to take in what Darrell was saying.

"What we do sounds far-fetched, I'm sure. Don't get caught up in the technology part. What has really made Inmel successful is the execution of our plan. Some of these same principles, if applied to *your* company, could help you change that Benfold buyout scenario to this one."

At that moment, a holographic image of Joe appeared. "At Chiron, we offer our customers and partners the very latest innovations in robotics. . . ." Darrell cut the connection with a snap of his fingers. "That's Chiron's Web site from the future, Joe. Pretty cool, huh? In this scenario, you have global reach and are a key player in transforming your industry. You have also changed the lives of people with disabilities worldwide with your robotics technology. Showing you more isn't important. What counts now is what you do next."

"How do we get there?" Joe asked, with so much enthusiasm that he surprised himself. "Chiron can become the innovator I always pictured it could be? Tell me more about that, Darrell."

"Maybe we'll have time for that later. I've shown you two possible directions for your company, and there are others. The question becomes, what will you do with the knowledge you are receiving? That will make all the difference."

"I'd like to know more about this Right Execution idea and how you see it working in my business."

"The first Right Execution principle is to *involve your whole organization in strategy and implementation plans and then create a culture of excellence.* Most organizations have a plan and set goals. What we've found is that many companies involve only the management team in planning and implementation."

Darrell leaned in and continued, "At Inmel, we get input from the whole company; we bring hundreds of people together in person and by teleconference for this purpose, plus key stakeholders, like outsourcing partners, customers, and outside consultants. Everyone gets a chance to share their ideas about how we can get from where we are to where we want to be. We can make many changes on the spot, in real time. How do you go about planning in *your* company, Joe?"

"We just send the management team off-site to set goals. Then we ask each management team member to handle his or her part."

"What kind of success have you had with that?"

"Mixed, really. Early on, it worked pretty well. As we got larger, the process was much less effective."

Darrell continued, "After we have our planning sessions, I conduct ongoing business reviews on a regular basis, and I expect that our management team and team leaders do so as well. We discuss expectations, what's working, and what's not. I've found that this ongoing dialogue sets a tone. People who work here know that accountability and high performance are priorities. We have set up our reward and recognition system to support high performance as well."

"Doesn't that take a lot of your time, though?"

"Honestly, Joe, I couldn't afford *not* to do it. It's a discipline that should be part of everything you do. This stuff really works if you do it consistently.

"The second Right Execution principle is to *hold people accountable for their personal and team objectives and give them the space to innovate.* Who are the people who are innovating in *your* organization, and how do you support them?"

"We haven't done a very good job of that, I guess. Tony and Sam helped us build the business through their experience and ability to innovate. As I look back on it now, I don't think we did enough to show our appreciation. I made a lot of money on their backs. I'm only sorry that we didn't handle things better with them."

"What could you have done to recognize and honor Tony and Sam for their contribution?" Darrell prodded.

"Well, I gave them bonuses here and there. George and I were more generous when the business was growing and still small. When we got larger, it became harder to just pick out certain people for rewards. Once in a while we discussed rewarding innovation in our management meetings, but like so many things that are important but not an emergency, we let it slide."

"Can you see what your role might be now, to help Chiron with Right Execution?"

"Maybe giving direction? And getting more involved with how things are implemented. And holding people accountable for what they've agreed to."

"Those are all important," Darrell nodded. "Definitely. And there are some other responsibilities that I've found necessary to leading and executing. One role of a leader is to create culture change, to create an environment in which people do well and excellence is expected.

"A leader must also influence, must provide a context and framework for making decisions and taking action. We want *everyone* to take ownership. If you don't influence others to want to take responsibility, then everybody loses.

"Another critical role I see for a leader of Right Execution is modeling whatever is essential to your organization's success. If there is a discrepancy between what you say and what you do, executing with excellence is impossible. My intentions and actions must be in alignment with what we've agreed is important, and that includes living the values. If I can't *be* and *do* what I expect from others, then I shouldn't be in a leadership role."

Joe felt his face flush as he replayed in his mind how inconsistent he'd been in his leadership style. Just last week he had gotten angry when Jose pointed out that Joe sometimes set a double standard. "You ask for participation," Jose had said. "And then you monopolize a meeting if the discussion isn't going in the direction you want." When Jose started to give Joe some examples of this behavior, Joe abruptly walked out of his office.

"Is this hitting close to home?" Darrell asked. Joe smiled sheepishly and waved for Darrell to continue.

"There's a third principle of Right Execution, and, personally, I believe it's the most meaningful: widen your view, understand what's important to you, and live your legacy."

Darrell could see from Joe's eyes that he was lost in thought. "What's going on in your head, Joe?"

"I was remembering when Tony and Sam introduced the idea of partnering with another organization to use our integrative robotics technology with people who have physical disabilities. They were so excited about applying our advances to help others."

"What happened?"

"I told them that I liked where they were heading. Unfortunately, we didn't do anything to support them. The idea died of neglect."

"At Inmel, we go back to the mission, vision, values, and core focus—what Robert told you about—to make sure a new idea fits. That's how we 'widen our view.' Like you, we see the positive effects technology could have on people with physical challenges. Doing something larger than ourselves has become essential to who we are as a company and to who we are as individuals.

"When I coach others about defining what's important in their lives, I ask them, 'What will it take for you to feel that you have had a successful life?' Ultimately, real and enduring success is about seeing the sum total of the activities and events in your life in an affirming and fulfilling way.

"When I think about my priorities and the priorities of others in my life, I see three areas of satisfaction: happiness, achievement, and legacy.

"Happiness is about what brings you joy. This can be spending time with your family, outdoor activities, or spiritual growth. Achievement deals with whatever you want to excel at or accomplish in your life. Perhaps you want to run in the Boston marathon, take your company public, or master a language. Legacy concerns what I like to call 'going from success to significance.'

"Legacy is the impact of the gift you want to leave behind. Your legacy might be a book you've written, a foundation you've started, or the people who have grown as a result of being around you. I believe that part of *my* legacy is living my values every day despite challenges. *Who I am* in every moment can have a significant impact on others and, ultimately, the world."

"You are very wise, Darrell," Joe said quietly.

"Ask yourself, 'What's enough for me?'" Darrell suggested. "Sometimes high achievers like you, Joe, want to be the best in *every* category. That isn't possible. You can achieve or become almost anything you want in life, but not all at once. Adjusting your expectations and defining what's 'just enough' for you brings fulfillment and balance."

Joe sat analyzing his current situation. Everything in his life now seemed to fall into the category of *achievement* and under the subcategory of *work.* "No wonder my family is so angry with me," Joe thought. "Maybe this is why I feel so empty inside."

As Darrell stood quietly, allowing Joe to absorb this concept, Joe's mind began to race. Suddenly he could envision a life in which, priorities plotted, he allowed himself time to enjoy his son's soccer games and take pleasure in spending time with family and friends. He felt a little giddy—maybe he could even work on that idea of legacy so all his hard work would live on in some way. He suddenly realized that the possibilities were boundless. Why had he never seen this before?

Aloud, he stated the obvious. "Um, my chart would be really lopsided if we were to graph my goals."

"And what do you think it will take for you to reconfigure your goals?" Darrell pressed.

"Oh, probably a car accident that stops me dead in my tracks," Joe smiled.

"So what's your legacy going to be, Joe?" Darrell asked.

Suddenly, sleep overtook Joe again.

FOCUS

THE RIGHT ROAD

Joe thought he had found the Right Road, only to have a near-death experience that clearly showed him how off-course he really was. How did Joe get so far off the Right Road? More important, how can you find the Right Road sooner rather than later without going through a divorce, a nasty business split, financial ruin, or even a near-death experience?

Joe's story is a composite of true-life stories many private company CEOs have shared with us over the past twenty years. Joe's story represents the transformation we have observed in so many of our clients who have gone from working "in" their businesses to working "on" them. Additionally, Joe's story points out how—if you take a more thoughtful look at yourself, where you are, and where you want to go—you can make the transition from what appears to be a successful life to a life of real significance for yourself and for others. That is the theme of this book.

What We Can Learn from Joe

Joe's story is about *how to loosen your hold on how you think things should be and how to create new possibilities in partnership with others.* Joe found himself with team members who wanted more responsibility, but he wasn't willing to give it to them. He also wasn't ready to share the economic benefits he gained from the innovation and hard work of others. Joe risked everything to have things his way at work and at home. As a result, he had lost touch with the needs and desires of some of the most important people in his life, including his wife, Sharon, and his son, Collin. Joe wanted to build a successful life, but he stubbornly held on to losing strategies. All those things that defined success and happiness for him seemed to be slipping away.

After Joe hit the tree and blacked out, he was visited by his old partner, George. From his vantage point, George could see that Joe was failing. George introduced Joe to three CEO mentors; these mentors took Joe to his past, present, and future and shared their observations and strategies on how Joe could transform his business and his life. They helped him realize that the best organizations and leaders understand the importance of Right Focus, Right People, and Right Execution, and that they implement these principles every day.

Successful CEOs who live fulfilling lives have learned strategies to create significance for their organizations and for themselves. During our research for this book, we interviewed more than fifty CEOs, who run primarily privately held, mid-size companies, about their success and the significance they feel they have created for themselves and for others. Their experiences offer a wealth of knowledge for businesspeople from the CEO to the entry-level manager. Internal and external consultants who work with leaders can also benefit from better understanding what top leadership thinks, feels, and finds important.

In Chapters 3 through 8, you will learn more about Right Focus, Right People, and Right Execution strategies and practices. You will also have the opportunity to tap into the wisdom and experience of the CEOs we interviewed for this book.

Right Focus, Right People, and Right Execution

Right Focus is centered on developing a mission, vision, and values for your company, yourself, and your family. It also includes determining your core focus: what you do best and have a passion for. Part of Right Focus is developing a plan to help you reach your vision and goals. We discuss how the top CEOs we interviewed have developed a Significance Plan that helps them frame decisions at work and at home as life gets more complicated and time gets more precious.

Right People is about how you select and/or hire those who will help you excel in your business and in your life. It's also about how you develop others. Right People includes everyone around you whom you care for and who care for you. They include your senior team and employees at work, your friends and family, your mentors, and your extended network of contacts that can serve as a source of inspiration, information, and support as you move through life. None of the top CEOs in our study had all the Right People in their life when they started out, although some counted their parents, grandparents, aunts and uncles, and other extended family as strong early mentors. They searched purposefully for the Right People or met them serendipitously over the years.

Right Execution focuses on executing with excellence and getting the right things done on time and with high impact. You will learn more about how to align yourself and your company with your plan and hold yourself and others accountable. Resiliency is a critical component of many of the CEO stories that you will read in the following chapters, particularly as it relates to execution. Very few of our top CEOs had a smooth path to creating significance in their lives. Building resiliency is a key success component.

Visit our Web site, www.ceoroadrules.com; you'll find a wide array of tools and techniques we've developed over the years in our executive coaching, consulting, and wealth management businesses that will help you live the life you truly want. Whether you are building on your existing strengths in the areas of Right Focus, Right People, or Right Execution, or are trying to figure out ways to make the areas that are a challenge for you better, we are confident that the information presented here will enable you to enjoy the ride!

CHAPTER 3

THE RIGHT FOCUS

Right Focus defines your organization's direction, helping you determine how you'll treat each other and how you'll get where you want to go. The principles that follow provide a framework so that people in your company can work toward a common goal within a culture they trust. Interestingly, when we asked our CEOs about their greatest accomplishment at the helm of their company, more than half of them stated that what really mattered was staying true to their company's direction or achieving the organization's vision as a team.

Right Focus consists of defining your *mission, vision, values,* and *core focus,* or what your organization can be best at. Let's look at each in detail.

Mission

The *mission* of an organization involves its purpose. Your mission answers questions such as, "Why are we here?" and "Why do we exist?" Mission is your organization's higher calling and ideally offers a sense of purpose or meaningful direction to each team member.

The challenge is to find a mission that is big enough, real enough, and inspiring enough to unite those in your organization so they feel they are a part of something larger than themselves. Mission ties what people in the organization enjoy doing and are good at to a clear direction. In short, an organization's mission is a touchstone that reminds a company about its essence.

Consider the following real-life mission statements, and notice how they have the ability to inspire people to do more than just collect a paycheck.

- "We help people achieve their goals, advance their careers, and enrich their lives through education." (RedVector, an e-learning company)
- "To improve quality of life through compassionate health care." (Surgery Partners, Inc.)
- "To help our clients achieve economic success and financial security." (BB&T Banks)

When developing a mission, organizations that involve all employees or a cross section of stakeholders who represent the company's diversity in the mission planning process are more likely to engage the majority of the people in the company sooner. Companies often do this by holding a series of meetings or retreats to have a dialogue about the organization's real purpose. But these successful companies don't stop there. On an ongoing basis, they encourage discussion and debate about whether the decisions the organization makes are in line with its broader mission.

For example, one of Mary's clients, the Florida Communication Group (FCG), owns a newspaper, a TV station, and an Internet news business. After holding a series of retreats for the leadership teams across all three businesses, the company defined its mission as "We enrich lives, build community, and fuel democracy." The company uses this higher purpose to assess whether the organization's strategies and day-to-day decisions are in alignment with its ultimate direction. As FCG's president, Ron Redfern, commented, "Our purpose is about the impact we can have on the lives of our customers and, even bigger, on democracy in our community, state, and country. With our mission firmly in place, we can remind ourselves whenever we get off purpose."

Be extra conscious when determining your mission so that you do not drive your organization with a limiting purpose—such as, to make money—that destabilizes your personal life, your health, and the personal lives of the team you're leading. Whether stated explicitly or implied, the idea of making money or beating the competition can be a negative driver as a mission, because employees may feel that a select few will benefit from the sweat of the many. Furthermore, it does not express a higher purpose, which is a core element of a good mission statement.

You are more likely to keep great people when you have a mission larger than yourself—one that also encompasses your personal mission. One of Dennis' business associates and a CEO we interviewed is a great example of matching his personal and business missions. After working with consulting firm Bain & Co. and learning the ropes on hundreds of projects, Michael Dougherty was offered and accepted a management position with a major publisher. While there, Michael found himself drawn to children's books and learning, and he built up significant expertise in those areas. All along he knew that something related to children's learning was his passion.

Through his contacts, Dougherty was offered the opportunity to head an entrepreneurial company that focused on children's education. He found alignment with his personal passion when he later became CEO of Kindermusik International, one of the leading early childhood education companies with teachers all over the world. "The company's focus is to change the world, teaching one child at a time," explains Dougherty. This company charge reflects the highly personal nature of Kindermusik classes in contrast to mass education. Not surprisingly, Kindermusik has prospered under Dougherty's leadership, won numerous awards for its educational products, and won a national award for its best practices as an employee-owned enterprise. By having this alignment, Dougherty has created fulfillment for himself and success for the organization.

When you have a strong mission and it aligns with that of the leadership of the organization, you and your organization are on the way to creating significance for your customers and for yourselves.

Vision

A critical part of Right Focus is *vision,* because it describes your preferred future and becomes your overriding goal. Vision answers questions such as, "Where do we see ourselves going?" and "Where do we want to be in the next five to ten years?" A vision differs from a mission in that the mission statement describes the essence of the organization and is not an overriding goal that, once achieved, changes. Mission statements usually last for the life of the company. The vision sets a direction you can track and measure; once reached, you must create a new vision to help the company grow (Collins and Porras 1997).

The first step in developing a vision is to bring together key stakeholders in the organization to reflect on the most positive future they can see for the company.

Mary asked FCG's leadership team: "If you were transported ten years into the future and your highest wishes for this organization were realized, what would you see?" She walked the group of sixty-eight people through a guided imagery exercise, asking them to picture themselves touring the organization, noticing what was going on and what they had accomplished over the ten years.

Before discussing their observations, each person wrote a specific and vivid description of exactly what he or she saw—no matter how far-fetched. Next, in groups of eight to ten, each person shared his or her vision of the future. This process promoted a thoughtful dialogue about what each participant visualized. The groups then summarized the common themes across the vision descriptions they heard, and then shared these "vision themes" with the large group. Some common themes revolved around what the workplace would look like, what customers would be experiencing, the company's growth, collective learning, the company's impact on society, winning awards, and being voted a great place to work. Such an exercise enables everyone to find "common ground" (Weisbord and Janoff 1995) on which to relate and build a compelling vision.

Involving others in developing a vision is important, because your team helps you shape an attractive and successful future for the company, and this creates mutual ownership in the company's success. In the end, the vision themes need to culminate in one overriding goal that summarizes where you'll be if your vision becomes reality. We call crafting this overriding goal writing the "headline" for all the common themes outlined as part of the future direction.

The "headline," or vision statement, for FCG became "Every Home, Every Day."

At this point, you must be careful, because your vision statement can become just a slogan if you don't make it something you can measure. That is, you have to make the overriding goal something you can break into intermediate goals that over time will get you to the final goal, or your vision.

For FCG, "Every Home, Every Day" means connecting with each customer in a specific geographic area at least once each twenty-four hours, either through the newspaper, the TV station, or the Internet news site. Preferably, there would be multiple daily customer contacts across the various platforms. FCG has targeted specific demographics that they want to penetrate and have set specific benchmarks to measure movement toward their vision.

In summary, your vision is the overall umbrella that answers the question, "What are we going after?" This big "what" gets broken down across departments in the organization so that goals and objectives relate back to the vision. Why is this process so important? Think about a time when you did your work with abandon—it just felt great to be working on a certain project or direction.

Time seemed to fly. Do you have a picture in your mind of this happening? When there's a clear, agreed-on picture of where you want to go, and you find the right people to work on this preferred future, employees will be engaged, because the work is interesting, it helps achieve a goal, and they have the freedom to approach the task their own way as long as there is agreement on the parameters and the end result.

How do you know that you have selected the right vision? Try taking this "vision litmus test" (Nanus 1995) by asking,

- Is your vision future oriented?
- Can your vision inspire enthusiasm and commitment?
- Does your vision set a standard of excellence?
- Is the vision ambitious enough? Not too ambitious?
- Is your vision unique to your company?
- Can you communicate your vision often with passion?

If you answered "yes" to each question, you're on the right road. If you answered "no" to even one question, go back and fine-tune your vision.

You can apply the litmus test to a variety of settings and organizations. For example, Gene Corrigan, former CEO of the Atlantic Coast Conference, one of the premier athletic conferences in the country, is also the former president of the NCAA. While president of the NCAA, Corrigan's vision was to "return the games to the student-athlete," which meant making sure that the athlete's ability to compete was balanced with being able to get an education that would see the person through life long after his or her postcollegiate athletic career was over. It also meant balancing big money sports such as basketball and football with less visible sports such as lacrosse, tennis, and golf for both men and women.

"This was a tough vision to stay true to," says Corrigan. "We had pressure on our athletes from professionals to leave college early; the 'arms race' as colleges competed with each other for state-of-the-art facilities, coaches, and athletes; and intense emphasis on money in various high-profile sports, which tended to overshadow academic achievements. We may have had limited success in the areas where other influences are strong, but we did our best to keep the balance, and we helped our colleges and universities build marvelous programs that have exceeded our vision in many sports, particularly the women's sports. If you have a strong vision, and execute only half of it well, you can still succeed beyond your and others' wildest imagination."

Some of the best CEOs we interviewed had a personal vision that lined up with their company's vision. Bruce Bodaken, the CEO of Blue Shield of California, sees both the vision of the company and his personal vision as creating social change for health care. Although this vision puts his organization in a minority position, as most health insurance companies advocate privately purchased policies or government programs, Bodaken advocates a public-private universal health-care plan and sees his company as leading the way for increasing access to good health care for everyone.

"I've always been a social activist and got into health care accidentally by taking a position that was offered to me," Bodaken says. "Once I did, the field aligned well with my vision and values. We provide a service that is so fundamental to human life, so necessary. Had it been a grocery store, I don't think that I could be as effective." Bruce favors legislation that supports universal insurance coverage; this outer-edge position is exhilarating to many because they see themselves as trendsetters who have a viable solution to the difficult problem of increasing availability of health-care insurance to the public.

To determine your *personal* vision, consider the following questions:

- Describe your personal and work life now (situation at work, home, how you spend your time, current goals, and so on).

- Describe what your personal and work life would be like in five to ten years if your highest wishes were realized. (If success were assured, what would your life look like?)

- What are the common themes in your description(s) of your life in five to ten years? What is the overriding goal or headline?

Unlike a mission statement, which describes your personal or organizational purpose, a vision statement for your organization, or for yourself, sets a standard or an overriding goal that you aspire to. Once that goal is fulfilled, it's critical to formulate a new, compelling vision statement. In 1961, John Kennedy announced his goal of sending an American safely to the moon before the end of the decade. That was an inspiring vision that NASA could visualize and benchmark. Some say that when that vision was achieved, the space program floundered because there wasn't another vision developed to take its place.

Values

We can define *values* as your core set of guiding principles, a code of ethics that cannot be compromised for financial gain—no matter what.

The difference between an average organization and a great one is its ability to answer the questions "What do we stand for?" and "Which values do we embrace?" Answering these questions honestly gets at your company's values.

Defining your values can be a participative process that involves a cross section of the entire company. One way to accomplish this involvement is to bring together stakeholders to outline value themes that have been part of the organization's culture, as well as desired value themes that are important to its future. Value themes are general descriptions of each value and usually need wordsmithing before you have a finished product. Identifying value themes is the forerunner to defining an organization's final set of core values.

First, agree on the top three to five value themes, such as integrity, customer focus, collaboration, innovation, and excellence. Then organize a values task force whose responsibility is to further define the value themes. Get a diverse cross section of people from all parts and levels of the organization. The task force will develop and discuss values definitions, go out into your organization to find out what others think, and recommend a specific set of core values. For example, at FCG the Values Task Force defined the organization's values as:

- *Integrity:* Be fair, be honest, and do the right thing.
- *Customer focus:* Exceed customer expectations.
- *Collaboration:* Working together makes us stronger.
- *Innovation:* Dare to think big and then make it happen.
- *Excellence:* Never be content with less than your best.
- *Diversity:* Reflect our communities in all we do.

Sometimes our CEOs had built the organization on specific established values. Usually these values reflect the CEO's personal values. Therefore, some of the CEOs we've worked with and interviewed didn't see the need to develop a new set of values; instead, they simply communicated their values in everything the company did.

For example, Dougherty at Kindermusik has three core values that he emphasizes in his business, with his family, and in working on community projects: Be Open, Honest, and Direct—or OHD for short. His board, executives, co-workers, and family hear one or all three mentioned just about every week. Dougherty speaks of these values frequently and gives examples of how they are being used and how they are not. As a result, everyone around him on a daily basis and the thousands of teachers worldwide who meet him or talk to him on the phone know his values and often respond by being more open, honest, and direct in their dealings with him and his company than they might otherwise have been.

Once you are clear about your and the company's values, make sure they don't conflict. For example, a personal value might be independence, while the organization's stated value might be participation and consensus building. You could feel frustrated on a regular basis if you prefer to make decisions more independently than the culture of the company dictates. If the CEO sends a mixed message, inconsistencies will become amplified throughout the company. A worst-case example would be a CEO who said that integrity was a core value of his company, while his top salespeople watched him lie to customers regarding problems with a product.

One way to ensure that the organization lives its values is to build them into the accountability system of

TABLE 1 | **Performance Values**

WHAT (Goals)	HOW (Behavior)
To attract and retain top talent	*Integrity:* Do the right thing
To develop a new offering that combines our core competencies with customer feedback	*Innovation:* Dare to think big and make it happen
To reach our net revenue goal of X	*Customer focus:* Exceed customer expectations

your organization. The best accountability systems focus on measuring high performance and include two major parts of performance: the "what," or the goals, and the "how," or the behaviors. When you take the vision headline and break it into goals, you get the "what" of performance; when you take the values and break them into behaviors, you get the "how" of performance. For a general representation of these, see Table 1.

In reality, you must define the behaviors even more specifically so that everyone is clear about what that value means. Value behaviors are those things everybody in the company will do if they are living the values. So the value behaviors related to integrity might look like this:

- Be honest and fair in all our interactions.
- Be true to our word; follow through on promises.
- Make decisions based on our values.
- Hold ourselves accountable.
- Be accessible.
- Do the right thing.
- Give and receive open and honest feedback.
- Take responsibility for our actions.
- Admit mistakes; don't stretch the truth.

Define your core values by developing value behaviors to better hold every individual in your company accountable for "how" they work. The best companies we've consulted with build their values into the organization's performance appraisal system, and, more important, they give regular feedback to each other on the use or misuse of the values.

Al Bodford runs a major transportation company. He has three core values: integrity, treating one another and customers well, and taking a proactive approach. He lives these values in every business decision he makes and finds ways to talk about these values in company meetings and newsletters. As Bodford explains, "Recently, a manager was reactive rather than proactive with a customer and compounded the problem by justifying his response as typical for the industry." Bodford, along with the manager's direct supervisor, discussed both mistakes with the individual and made sure the experience became a learning lesson for all managers by publicly talking about the discrepancy between the values and their actions and also by showing others what some proactive alternatives might be. To his credit, the manager in question went back to the customer with a new approach and the customer in turn appreciated the "going-the-extra-mile" attitude enough to increase business with the company.

Values are the philosophy of your company and should reflect the culture as well as the priorities in terms of how you will treat your customers, stakeholders, and each other. By holding others accountable, not only for the results but also for how they were attained, you reinforce your values and incorporate them into the fabric of your company.

Core Focus

To determine your *core focus,* consider the answer to the question "What can we be best at in *our* world?" It positions your company to excel in a core area that gives you a competitive advantage and allows you to focus your resources on what you're best at.

In his outstanding book *Good to Great,* Jim Collins outlined this same principle as part of what he called "the Hedgehog Concept." Basically, the Hedgehog Concept states that when the following three intersecting ideas are active within a company, performance consistently goes from good to great. The three are:

- Passion for what you're doing (mission and values)
- A viable economic engine or business model
- A focus on what you can be best in the world at (vision and core focus)

These observations dovetail with what we've observed in our interviews and in our work with privately held company CEOs. Our only caveat is that Collins talks about a superlative "best in *the* world," and we have found that with our CEOs the description "best in *our* world" is more accurate and realistic.

When they asked themselves, "What can we be best at in our world?" FCG leaders resisted picking one thing, since this division of the company is made up of a newspaper, a TV station, and an Internet news business. But after doing a lot of talking and exploring options, they found that by defining their core focus and putting resources behind it, they were able to grow in ways they had never imagined.

FCG decided its core focus was "to converge all three enterprises to offer our customers a unique mix of services that our competition can't." FCG's core focus, or what it can be best at in its world, is the convergence of the three businesses to integrate media in a unique way. The core focus strategically supports the company's vision of "Every Home, Every Day" in that this blending enhances the chances that the target market will respond to the one-of-a-kind crossover coverage by newspaper reporters, newscasters, and news on the Internet.

Your core focus is more than your business model; it asks you to define what you can excel at and where you can build your competence. With a clear and compelling mission, vision, values, and core focus, your company has a strong foundation on which to grow and become more than you imagined. In the next chapter you will learn how to build on this foundation by using Right Planning.

•

Our top CEOs all have defined their specific mission, vision, values, and core focus. How about you?

•

What are *you* passionate about? Not what your parents, spouse, best friend, management team, or anyone else thinks you should be passionate about, but what you enjoy doing that causes you to lose all track of time.

•

Passion about your life and career will inevitably lead to success and happiness. CEOs who figure out their life's passion sooner are more fulfilled and have more fun working than their less engaged counterparts do. What would your company need to look like so you would spring out of bed in the morning, looking forward to the challenges of the day?

•

Be satisfied when you find your passionate niche and don't jump to a new leadership opportunity just because big bucks dangle in front of you. Those who fall for the siren song of easy money almost universally find themselves falling back and having to work double-time to get back on their Right Road.

•

A sense of commitment will enable your company to progress toward an overriding goal or inspiring vision. Share your dreams with your team and family, and feel the powerful force that will begin to move you swiftly ahead.

•

Develop a vision that is compelling to those who will carry it out. Then do everything in your power to stay true to the vision and communicate it to internal and external people every chance you get.

•

Take time to clarify what your values are and notice how they play out in your day-to-day activities at your company and at home. Rectify any inconsistencies and model what you preach.

•

It's easy to get scattered: **find your core focus** and stick to it. Develop good habits to avoid distractions.

•

What do you want to be remembered for? It probably won't be last quarter's financial results. Are you working on a life that is larger than yourself?

CHAPTER

4

THE RIGHT PLANNING

Right Planning is an essential aspect of Right Focus.
Remember that Right Focus provides a road map, con-
sisting of a mission, vision, values, and core focus. Now
it's time to consider some specific internal and external
factors for both your personal life and your business. You
can combine these internal and external factors into a
"Significance Plan," which will enhance your chances of
creating a life you and those you care about can look
back on with pride and a feeling of fulfillment.

A Significance Plan

The *internal aspect* of significance planning encompasses
your dreams, vision, and goals as determined by what

significance means to you, your family, and perhaps even your friends. For some of our top CEOs, such planning also encompasses what significance means to the team at work and to the community. You mapped out some internal factors in the previous chapter, when you determined your personal mission, vision, and values.

The *external aspect* encompasses the more traditional business and personal financial planning, which are equally important to your Right Focus and your Significance Plan, and which we'll cover later in the chapter.

Suppose your life plan consists of the following factors.

- Build a business that makes you financially independent
- Have a great relationship with your spouse and network of friends
- Live in a great home
- Travel to fun places and enjoy luxuries
- Raise several children who do well in school and life
- Live a good life in which you enjoy most days
- Contribute to society in some way

Can't lose with this combination, right? That's what many CEOs we interviewed thought . . . until they faced the tough reality that giving 110 percent to any one of these areas, especially your business, often destabilizes the other areas. A good Significance Plan puts on paper what you feel and think will make you successful in all areas of your life, and which of those possibilities you will regret losing if they end up in the ditch.

A Balanced and Focused Plan

Combining business and personal planning is one of the toughest challenges CEOs face. For the CEOs we interviewed, just juggling a busy work schedule, connecting at a deeper level with a spouse or significant other, getting to their kid's soccer games, and keeping themselves in some kind of physical shape requires a good daily and weekly plan.

Kindermusik's Dougherty found the right balance: a fun, dynamic, and profitable business to run; a nice place to live; and an active, stimulating lifestyle to balance his life. "It was tough at first when we moved from San Francisco to Greensboro, North Carolina. On the surface, San Francisco appeared to have so much more to offer in terms of a stimulating and resourceful work and living environment. But the opportunity to run a company that lined up so well with my personal mission and interests was too attractive to let go. This move wound up affording me and my family a life-changing experience that I didn't anticipate. I now run a successful business totally in sync with my skills and values, we are in the center of wonderful culture, and my wife and I love the family-friendly environment in Greensboro. I coach my kid's soccer team and feel like everything in my life is in much better balance."

Think you're facing too many variables to do good planning, much less your Significance Plan? Turns out many planning challenges are similar from company to company and industry to industry. Many of the CEOs we talked with admitted they didn't plan much early on in their careers because they thought it wouldn't be fruitful given their set of challenges.

Later in their lives, many CEOs look back with the realization that they won the marathon but lost way too many races along the way because they didn't plan or they planned poorly. Many of the CEOs we surveyed wished they had, first, done *more* planning *sooner;* second, done more *thoughtful* planning with better research; and, third, thought in terms of combining personal and business plans to guide decision making. Southchem's former CEO Joe Collie revealed: "We built our business a brick at a time. We probably did more and better planning than our competitors, which is one of the reasons why we succeeded. In hindsight, we didn't do nearly as much planning as we should have. My favorite saying is 'If you don't have a plan, any road will get you there.' The problem is 'there' may not be where you would like to be!"

Collie learned to not just do some planning but to also think about his Significance Plan every step along the way. Following is Collie's vision of significance, which he incorporated into his internal and external plans to "live the life that really matters."

- *Have a loving family.* He and his wife, Barbara, raised a family whose members love and support each other despite the usual family squabbles that happen from time to time.

- *Raise children who have both brains and street smarts.* Two of his three children cut their teeth in his business and moved on to their own passions after the business was sold. All three children have demonstrated abilities to adapt and succeed in good times and bad.

- *Build a strong business doing what I love with employees who share the vision and the profits.* Joe built a great business and a great team and was generous in his sharing of himself and profits. The new owner of the business kept most of the original team.

- *Give back to the community.* Joe and Barbara have made significant contributions in time, effort, and money to their community and church, serving on numerous boards. They have also set up charitable trusts and foundations to continue their good works long after they have died.

- *Live life with integrity, empathy, and passion.* From being a part of the Normandy invasion in WWII to being a courageous business leader to being a good father and husband, Joe has walked the talk and, at age eighty, has accomplished most of his Significance Plan.

Why Planning Matters

You may consider yourself to be the classic "ready-fire-aim" type of leader, who seems to do little planning and works off a piece of paper in his back pocket or scribbles a new business scheme on a napkin at a restaurant. It's possible to be successful with a fire-before-you-aim approach, if you still do your homework on your competitors and their market niche and work your rear end off along the way. You may have problems, however, growing your company and transfering your well-honed instincts to new employees. It's naturally harder to have your key executives and staff connect to your vision when it's sitting in your back pocket. So make a plan!

Even those CEOs who do not formally plan *all* aspects of their career and personal lives believe planning must play a major role at key moments: becoming CEO, moving the company to a higher level, or getting their life balanced so they can connect better with family and ultimately with their personal passions.

Sheldon Jacobs, retired CEO of a West Coast engineering company, mentors young entrepreneurs in the dos and don'ts of building a company. "If they are smart, have passion, a vision, and guts, they'll succeed up to a point with poor planning," says Jacobs. "Show me a young CEO who combines these traits with a living, dynamic plan, and there you've usually got the next multimillion-dollar enterprise."

Sometimes Looking Back to Move Forward

Over half of the CEOs in our survey found themselves at some point repeating the mistakes of their youth but were able to make solid, life-changing adjustments along the road, or they made radical transformations to move toward the life balance they sought. Our top CEOs were clear on this point: it is absolutely essential to address your baggage from the past before you can develop a top-notch Significance Plan.

John Lankins, an insurance company CEO, illustrates. "My family was a mess," he says. "I learned what not to do, but had to keep watching myself so I didn't fall into the dysfunctional habits that were my role models when I was young. These included failing to admit mistakes and apologize, telling people to do things and then doing the opposite, and cutting off communication when you didn't like what you were hearing.

"Another CEO friend of mine did the same type of planning I did, but he repeated most of the mistakes of his parents. He married a nice woman, but treated her poorly by not involving her in major family decisions and slowly sucking the life out of her own dreams by ignoring them. He raised kids who were not disciplined and they turned to drugs as they lost respect for their parents and their future. And he brought his anger at the world into work every day of his life. He tried to lose himself in his work, but he had a short fuse and ran off any good employee who disagreed with him or seemed to be living the happy life he wasn't. He never tried to get help, professional or otherwise. His plan failed and mine worked. I can't help but think the difference wasn't brains, but baggage."

Successful CEOs have focused business and personal plans and are able to adjust those plans as circumstances change around them. Both "nature" and "nurture" give them the skills to do this: many learned good coping and adjustment skills from their parents, either through positive role models or, in a surprising number of cases, negative role models. Dysfunctional families create daily learning exercises on how to be flexible, deal with irrational people and events, and generally stay positive. It is also true that demons from the past may drive someone to be more successful, but those demons may sow the seed of failure and impede the process of living the life that matters.

Becoming more conscious of some of the negative programs that play out in our lives is the first step in learning from past mistakes. Taking time to reflect and being brutally honest with yourself isn't easy. A key to personal and professional growth is having outside support and reprogramming self-defeating behaviors.

For example, Jerry Dale, CEO of a midwestern manufacturing company, was always on the go and rarely slowed down enough to realize that he was losing touch with his family. One day at lunch with his closest mentor, he confided that things weren't going great at home. He was fighting more and more with his wife and their intimacy was suffering, his son was talking less to him and getting into more trouble at school, and his sister, who he had been very close to, wasn't calling him every week just to talk anymore.

After digging deeper, he realized he was replaying his father's life story, which was still a source of pain for him and his mother. His mentor suggested he write down a short list of the three top items that his wife, son, and sister would love for him to do the very next week, and then implement the plan as if it was for his top customer. Jerry realized his family was his "top customer"; he just wasn't treating them that way. Jerry followed through on the list and, every Friday afternoon, made another list for the next week. After several months, it was a part of Jerry's routine and he had reprogrammed a potentially disastrous set of behaviors. Simple, but highly effective.

Past Baggage and How to Let Go

What if you're ready to create your Significance Plan, but recognize you still have some issues to deal with? How do you "pass go"? Our CEO group most often cleared their mental roadblocks in the following ways.

- *Having mentors and close friends.* Opening up and talking over the past, however painful, is one of the most often mentioned ways the top CEOs cleared out the cobwebs to produce good Significance Planning. You may be surprised just how many seemingly highly successful people had to deal with the past to get where they are now. A consistent pattern that we've seen with CEOs who excel is their ability to choose and surround themselves with healthy and successful mentors and friends; these choices can make all the difference between getting dragged down by someone else's baggage and learning new ways to handle tough situations.

- *Having a great life partner.* Next most often mentioned is finding the right life partner. Such partners helped the CEOs we spoke with deal with past nightmares and become mentally healthy and confident. Realize that most people don't "sign up" to fix a partner with baggage, so if you have some really tough issues, combine self-work and therapy to strengthen your relationship. Remember also that if you help your partner find significance, you'll both be happier and healthier.

- *Having a CEO peer advisory board.* It's lonely at the top. Often it's difficult to get honest feedback from others, especially when they have a vested interest in your taking certain actions or realizing certain outcomes. Your CFO, spouse, significant other, or best friend may not be able to be objective when what you do will have a certain impact on their lives. Running issues by peers and getting the benefit of their collective experiences in a CEO forum can make a big difference in personal and business growth.

- *Having a therapist.* Older CEOs in our study used this option less frequently; younger CEOs were less hesitant, even scheduling quarterly "mental health checkups." Finding a compatible therapist may take a few tries. Other CEOs and leaders are often the best source of referrals. If you approach your network with the idea of building on strengths rather than fixing something that is broken, you'll be more likely to try this option and get better results.

Planning Via Scenario Learning

Don't underestimate the *power of thinking ahead* in an ever-changing and chaotic world. Top CEOs develop the skills to evaluate scenarios by a variety of methods, such as studying both winners and losers in history's struggles and triumphs, having parents or early mentors who stressed foresight, and having jobs in competitive industries that force them to be on top of their game.

The best CEOs can anticipate the next move in the game; every move changes the intelligent options going forward. Sometimes you can anticipate the exact sequence of moves and actions, but most of the time you have to adjust as you go, armed with a general vision of what will happen.

Scenario learning (SL) helps CEOs sharpen their ability to create a dynamic plan for the future. It helps them frame issues and keep within the guidelines of a broader Significance Plan. Scenario learning is distinguished from strategic planning in its emphasis on *learning.*

Shell Oil undertook one of the first large-scale SL projects in the United States in the late 1960s. The process let top executives foresee every major variable in the oil business that would unfold in the early 1970s, although the company barely adjusted its preplanning strategy. Shell's "Official Future"—the one that prejudices had imprinted in the executives' brains—was so strong that the company couldn't change to the Right Road even though it had a comprehensive plan mapped out and all the signs pointed to a different direction from the one it was taking. Shell Oil eventually did adjust, and because it had a plan mapped out, the company did it faster than the competition.

Shell's ability to adjust more quickly than its "seven sister" competitors catapulted Shell into a much stronger position in the oil industry. The company had already written the scripts, crafted the scene selection, and played the movie over and over, so when it saw the early scenes being played, it dropped right into its own role on the world stage. Former Shell executives we interviewed uniformly said they wished they had changed ahead of events, but when everyone else is locked into a similar official future, it's tough to buck the trend. Despite missing the huge opportunity to change direction ahead of time, they all credited scenario learning with helping them change faster with more purpose, while their competitors were still struggling with figuring out what happened.

You don't have to be a big public company like Shell to effectively use SL. In fact, it's often easier in smaller private companies, as long as you can slow your team down long enough to go through the process and you have the patience to let the bottom-up process of brain-storming and scenario creation work.

A small robotics firm run by one of our top CEOs developed four scenarios to try to answer three major questions: (1) What are the prospects for robotic manu-facturing in the United States versus overseas in the next three years? (2) Are our targeted systems and processes going to meet the amount and type of demand? and (3) How can we adjust our "permanent" employee mind-set to deal with the engineers needed under the various sce-narios? The four scenarios developed were the following.

- *Boom for overseas industry, bust for us.* This scenario assumes companies continue to trade workers for robots, but much of the facilities are placed overseas in markets where major competitors are already well established.

  - *Key ideas:* Develop stronger overseas presence and strategic alliances; monitor trends of outsourcing versus insourcing.

  - *Key question for the Significance Plan:* Key execu-tives have to travel considerably more, which may destabilize home lives. How do we minimize this?

- *Boom for U.S. industry, boom for us.* Companies in the United States continue to favor technology accelera-tors and U.S. dollar weakness, plus political factors see U.S. robotics gain major share.

  - *Key ideas:* We have the right processes and systems, but not enough experienced engineers; therefore,

develop a flex hiring system that fast-tracks training of permanent positions and uses specialized
temporary services to fill demand that we judge to
be nonpermanent.

- *Key question for the Significance Plan:* Our corporate culture is one of teamwork and sharing the
  profits. How well will temps and perms work side-
  by-side in this environment?

- *Boom for U.S. industry, technology changes playing
  field.* The U.S. market for robots booms but the types
  of systems change faster than our R&D system.

  - *Key ideas:* Develop a better system to track customer
    needs, even loaning engineers to customers as they
    are designing new systems. Create a fast-response team
    that will anticipate customer needs and demands.

  - *Key question for the Significance Plan:* Engineers
    working on shrinking technology may feel less
    important than those working on sexier projects.
    How do we keep our best people motivated in a
    changing environment?

- *Robotics plateau worldwide, zero job growth not toler-
  ated.* A scenario right from the headlines develops as
  more politicians here and overseas cave in to worker
  demands to protect jobs.

  - *Key ideas:* Enhances the need for a flex hiring sys-
    tem. Determine if efforts in above scenarios destabi-
    lize profitability of the overall firm.

  - *Key question for the Significance Plan:* In order to
    minimize the risks ahead and plan for growth, we
    may find ourselves jeopardizing bonuses of our core
    engineers. Will they think it was worth it?

With a good SL process, sometimes the best scenario leaps out as the most likely series of events, but this company found as much strength in the questions and how they were researched by multiple teams as they did in the answers. The company was able to get ahead of the curve on various strategies, preparing themselves for a lot of change in the process. As we'll discuss in the chapter on Right Resiliency, this may be one of the greatest gifts of the SL process!

Here are eight steps for creating scenarios, no matter what size your company is.

Step 1. *Identify the key issue or decision.* What keeps you up at night? This could include whether to grow internally or acquire other companies or both. It could also include how these strategies might affect your relationship with your family if it means you'll "disappear" for the next year.

Step 2. *What key factors may spell success or failure?* When looking at options for your key issue, what must you know? How will you define success or failure?

Step 3. *Determine the driving forces.* What are the forces behind your key factors? This is where good scenario learners do intensive homework and do their best learning. What are the major trends and, your real challenges, what could break each trend?

Step 4. *Rank factors and drivers by importance and uncertainty.* Identify the two or three trends and drivers that are key to your success and are most uncertain.

Step 5. *Create the scenario skeleton.* Use the results of step 4 to begin to form your main scenarios. Create three or four scenarios that use the key drivers, variables, and uncertainties in ways that will be productive to getting to the heart of your most urgent issue. Assign different scenarios to subgroups; then have one group take the best-case scenario, another the worst-case, a third the middle-of-the road scenario, and the fourth group a wild-card scenario.

Step 6. *Put muscle on the skeleton.* You'll begin to see the future form in each scenario. Adjust it as a good director would with a major motion picture.

Step 7. *Review your route.* Go back to the decision you're trying to make and see how it plays out in each scenario. If the road you originally thought looked good feels less comfortable now, go with your intuition and examine that road more carefully.

Step 8. *Develop a "dashboard" and check gauges for your scenarios.* In your car, speed and amount of fuel are the two critical variables you need to monitor, along with warning lights to tell you if something major is developing. By now you have probably figured out a few critical things to watch closely that will help you and your team figure out which scenario is unfolding. Spend some time on this and then make sure you and your team are watching the dashboard and discussing the "what" and the "why" as events unfold.

One CEO we interviewed created multiple scenarios at age fifty that included the following.

- Building his company to greater success over the next ten years and then selling it

- Dividing up the president and CEO duties immediately and building an internal team in five years so he can sell and pursue his dream of building racing yachts

- Promote one of his promising vice presidents and immediately begin working on the racing yacht dream one or two days a week

He overlaid these three scenarios with his family goals and current business plan. This SL exercise helped give him the clarity to pursue a vision that he admits would otherwise have been lost in the day-to-day business grind of his company.

The uses of SL are limited only by your imagination. SL can help you visualize different significance options and see how you like the ending, while you still have time to change the story line and the characters. SL is a wonderful tool in your pursuit of significance beyond success.

One of the consistent patterns that we've seen in the CEOs who lead innovative companies is the ability to see patterns and trends in their businesses and industries before others do. One of our CEOs recognized the opportunity in online learning for professionals who need continuing education credits from similar trends he had noticed in the computer business years earlier. He naturally uses SL in how he thinks about business development and growth and is building a company that is taking the lead in the markets it serves.

SL sharpens your mind and your intuition so that you can better anticipate patterns and trends and use them to your advantage.

External Planning for the Right Financial Road

Personal planning of your life finances is another key element of Right Planning. If you're going to create a well-integrated Significance Plan, this is where you will need to combine insightful *internal* planning (you and your family's dreams and goals) with high-quality *external* planning (cash flow, taxes, investments, and so on). Here are a few classic external planning ideas that can crush or contain your internal quest for significance.

- *"I'm finally making good money, so why stop?"* This single idea has caused many CEOs, as well as doctors and lawyers and other professionals, to stay on long after their passion for the business has waned. You may come out with more money at the end, but is it worth sacrificing one or more of your goals for significance?

- *"I've become a master at my craft, so why change?"* Does your work still get you excited? If so, maybe you're where you should be. Many of our most satisfied CEOs have held leadership roles in a number of diverse companies, including nonprofit entities, after they sold their businesses.

- *"I need to have a lot of money set aside, so I keep working and saving!"* This seems reasonable on the surface, but our happiest CEOs were more in the giving mode than the hoarding mode. The financial services industry has promoted the "save until it hurts" approach, not always for unselfish reasons. Think carefully through how much is enough with those you love.

- *"I need a good estate plan to save every dollar of tax possible."* Our top CEOs are tax savvy but also have spent the majority of their time planning their estate on nontax issues, such as how to keep the next generation motivated, teach their favorite charity to fish instead of giving them a fish, and communicate their significance plan to future generations.

One definition of economics is the allocation of scarce resources, which for many entrepreneurs in their early years means investing everything in the business. This early business development means they can't afford to cover all the normal financial plan contingencies, only those priorities most important to their long-range plan.

The typical evolution of external planning involves early, mid-, and high-success stages.

- *Early stage.* In this stage, the CEO has little savings, little need for tax planning, and big liabilities. Adequate life, health, disability, and liability insurance are important for both the business and the family. A simple "I love you" will is typical, with all assets going to the spouse and guardians named. The spouse is usually the beneficiary of life insurance proceeds. You may start funding custodial and/or 529 plans for future college education, unless you want your children to work for part of their keep in college.

- *Mid-stage.* Because the business is becoming valuable during this stage, you need to kick everything up several notches. Adequate insurance is still important, but now you must carefully plan your buyout, which may also require funding through more life insurance. Retirement plans are building up value, and you must give more thought to good asset allocation. Your will now needs a credit shelter or family trust and some thought on how larger sums of money might affect the lives of your children. You may need to put life insurance into an irrevocable trust to shelter it from estate taxes. Finally, you may be looking at buying your own building instead of leasing.

- *High-success stage.* The foundation built in the previous stages may need greater intensity of thought and techniques to not only build, but also protect value. Asset protection strategies become more important depending on your exposure. Personal investments are growing along with retirement assets, and professional guidance becomes more crucial. Your Significance Plan may now include the implementation of lifetime gifts or after-death bequests to your favorite charities. You probably have enough assets to last your lifetime, but making sure your business stays healthy is a priority, along with figuring out your exit strategy.

As you progress from the early stage to the mid-stage to the high-success stage, you need a multitude of things, such as a business plan; key advisors in various aspects of the planning (attorneys, accountants, financial advisors, and so on); and an investment, tax, and retirement plan. Many CEOs are familiar with these external items, but some are not. Even those who are familiar with the items can benefit from a refresher on the topics or an unbiased second opinion.

In their research on successful people who reported great satisfaction with their lives, Nash and Stevenson, authors of the book *Just Enough,* talk about the importance of life balance in goal setting. They state that because we have too many choices in our lives, our targets may shift and increase as more choices appear. Because so many accomplished people are achievement oriented in all they do, they often ignore or set standards that are too high to balance with other goals set.

Nash and Stevenson suggest and validate that those who ask themselves, "What's enough for me?" and apply this approach to four areas of their life, are in fact the most fulfilled. These four areas are *happiness* (what brings you pleasure or satisfaction in life), *achievement* (what accomplishments you are reaching for), *significance* (what positive impact you want to have on those you care about), and *legacy* (how you will build on your values to help others find future success). Within each area, the authors suggest you set goals in each of these categories: self, family, work, and community. So for example, under the *happiness* category of "family," you might include the ongoing goal of attending at least 75 percent of your

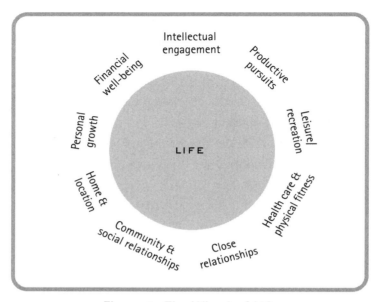

Figure 1 The Wheel of Life

daughter's soccer games; under the *achievement* category of "self," you might set a goal of running in a marathon; under the *significance* category of "work," you might set the goal of implementing a succession plan; and under the *legacy* category of "community," you might set the goal of starting a foundation in your community to support education of the underprivileged.

Another powerful tool is the "Wheel of Life," shown in Figure 1. The wheel enables you to visualize how well your life is balanced and also determine the areas of your life that might be "wobbling" and affecting your Significance Plan. It affords the opportunity to periodically reassess where you are in relation to where you want to be.

. The wheel has existed in various forms for more than thirty years. It has been refined and enhanced by several visionaries in the financial life planning field, notably Carol Anderson of Money Quotient and Pam Williams of Navigating Wealth.

The Wheel of Life helps you define nine key aspects of your life that, taken together, determine how successful your journey in life might be. Carol Anderson describes it this way: "Whether each of the nine areas is always at a level 10 or not is less important than the idea that a person's or a family's collective wheel is in balance and that there is positive progress throughout life."

A number of the private company CEOs we have interviewed have only recently been able to balance out their wheels. Some have had major challenges with marriages and children that caused problems in such areas as their fitness, stress level, and personal growth.

Pam Williams works with many Silicon Valley executives who constantly struggle to find balance between their personal and professional lives. According to Pam, "the Wheel of Life is a critical exercise for all CEOs to complete annually and revisit periodically with their spouse, family, and everyone who is important to them. It's such an easy exercise, yet so powerful. The wheel helps answer questions such as 'What trade-offs am I making for success?' The wheel also tracks where you are today and will help you navigate where you want to go tomorrow. It's a great way to start important conversations with children and grandchildren about how to establish life priorities. They will love having these conversations with you and having you share your wisdom."

We have developed a customized version of the Wheel of Life for executives that takes into account the unique challenges and opportunities leaders face. Another interesting way to use the wheel is to rank the nine areas at various turning points in your life, such as when you became an entrepreneur or when you faced a major crisis in your business. Discussing with others who are part of your support system how your wheel has changed over time can help you better understand your life dynamics and past patterns of behavior; this process also provides insight into areas that need attention now and in the future. If you would like to complete the interactive wheel exercise, go to www.ceoroadrules.com.

The process of Right Planning comes down to developing a Significance Plan that considers all internal and external aspects to produce success, significance, and satisfaction.

•

Find good advisors early on and take the time to map out your internal and external personal plan, paying attention to your Significance Plan. Then monitor the personal plan and shift gears as your company situation and business plan change.

•

Develop your vision of significance. Do this on your own, then with a key person such as your spouse or significant other; involve family members and key people in your business as appropriate. Would you better understand and relate to the people around you every day if you knew what *they* aspire to for significance in their lives?

•

Figure out what past baggage may be affecting your communication and relationships with your family, your work associates, your friends, and others you deal with every day. Take action to deal better with the baggage with the help of mentors, close friends, your life partner, CEO peer advisory boards, and counseling.

●

Consider various scenarios using the input of people you trust, including industry experts, mentors, advisors, and teammates when creating both your business and personal plans. Scenario projections in planning may spell the difference between the Right Road and a dead end. They can also help you develop the right balance with your Significance Plan.

●

Develop a "dashboard" with gauges that tell you how you are doing in both your business and personal life. Objective goals are easier to track than subjective ones. Set benchmarks with your life partner and family on what will constitute success and significance.

●

As you do traditional external business and personal planning, be true to your vision and set your own pace without the burden of the myths and distractions that swirl around you every day. Make sure your advisory team is talented, grows with you as you grow, is compensated in alignment with your best interests, and has an appreciation for the balance of internal and external planning so they both understand and help you achieve your Significance Plan.

●

Consider the four areas of happiness, achievement, significance, and legacy, and define what "just enough" is for you. To get more specific, use Nash and Stevenson's process of sorting by self, family, work, and community.

PART TWO

PEOPLE

THE RIGHT PEOPLE

Having the Right People on your team can spell the difference between success and failure. When it comes to *your* team, the Right People include (1) your work team, (2) your network and support team, and (3) your home team. Let's look at each team in detail so you can better understand how to enhance that area of your life. After all, without a complete and balanced team, your professional and personal performance will suffer.

Your Work Team

Private company CEOs usually build their organizational team incrementally as the company grows and can afford, and attract, better talent. The stakes are a lot higher earlier in the company's growth. Hiring the wrong person can very well put you out of business. One of the CEOs Mary works with reports several cases in which employees have stolen money from the company, including a creative CFO who, among other things, had all his family cars listed as company cars.

Having the Right People on your team takes work—to attract them and to keep them. We have seen some companies find the Right People only to lose them because of shortsightedness like Joe's, when he began to show indifference to Tony and Sam, who had helped build his company. Sometimes the company culture is at fault, rewarding the average performer and punishing the high performer. For example, a star performer might want to improve a product or service, but management doesn't listen to his or her ideas and views the employee as a troublemaker for being passionate about a product improvement. At the same time, those less caring employees who just do their job win promotions because they don't challenge the status quo.

As a private company grows to the next level of maturity, CEOs must institute policies, practices, and procedures to bring about consistency and operational effectiveness on a larger scale. When your organization might be going through this natural growth phase of establishing standards and norms, the high-performing innovators may feel disenfranchised by their more bureaucratic counterparts because they prefer the more entrepreneurial, free-wheeling environment of an early-stage company. When some companies become too bureaucratic, good people leave. We will speak more about reinforcing the right behaviors in Chapter 7, on Right Execution.

We can cite three main reasons why companies don't hire the right people.

- *Hastiness or operating from a sense of urgency that overrides good decision making.* Getting someone too quickly to fill a gap that suddenly got bigger with business growth is a frequently mentioned reason why organizations hire the wrong person. Many top CEOs admit candidly that they do some things very well, but sizing up new hires isn't always one of them. Hiring someone in haste winds up making more work for everyone, not to mention the backlash of picking someone who fails in a leadership role. Joe's head of manufacturing, Tom Trout, is an example of how hiring the wrong manager can have an impact far beyond what anyone imagined.

- *Poor fit.* The hiring company often doesn't have a way to *effectively* find, attract, and select top talent. We have seen organizations spend precious hours cleaning up hiring messes and in proportion very little time on thinking through their selection and hiring process. The selection process should start with getting clarity on the roles and responsibilities of the position you want to fill. To do so, answer the following:

  - What are the key skills, competencies, and experience this person will need?

- How will we assess whether the candidates' values align with the company's?

- How will we reach this kind of talent so we have a solid pool of candidates to choose from?

- *The selection process isn't systematic and measures the wrong things.* You position yourself for improved hiring when you set up a selection process that systematically screens candidates for skills, competencies, and past experiences that contribute to being effective in the target position and company culture. Ideally, if your organization is living the values it professes, your culture is a reflection of the values in action. Culture fit can also take the form of how comfortable someone feels with being proactive in a company that doesn't have a lot of established policies. One of the mistakes that many of our private-company clients have made is hiring someone from a large public company who is used to having lots of resources available, only to find that the new hire can't get used to the more entrepreneurial environment in which he or she is expected to be proactive, resources are less plentiful, and there is less structure in place to guide actions.

Evaluation of Candidates

If you want the Right People, you must have at the core of your approach the following guiding principle: *past behavior speaks volumes about future behavior.* Yes, people can change; however, change rarely occurs unless some major crisis or demand for change comes about due to external circumstances, such as being fired, a major illness, or an accident. That's why you must find a way to ferret out information about the candidates' past successes and failures and see how these fit the opportunity at hand. Gather focused information to paint a realistic picture of the candidates' strengths and weaknesses. Corroborate your findings through interviews with references and other assessments you might use.

One of the factors that sets some companies apart from others is the preparation they put into the design of their interview. Mary has taught clients how to conduct behavior-based interviews in which the focus is on defining a position by breaking it into competencies and behaviors. A position can involve four to ten competencies on average. An example of a competency is *judgment*. Once you have the competency defined, you can list important actions and behaviors that support that competency. Consider the following example.

Judgment
Recognizes and weighs alternatives; considers risks, resources, and constraints prior to making a commitment or decision

Important Actions and Behaviors
- Considers the impact of various choices on different people and the situation
- Evaluates the risks and takes risks involved in making specific decisions
- Looks at/for alternatives

- Applies organization's values to each situation
- Anticipates the impact of decision options
- Assesses alternatives to anticipate the goodness of fit
- Involves those with a stake in the situation and decision making to keep them in the loop

Next, use the CAR—*Circumstance,* or example; *Action,* or response; and *Result,* or outcome—approach to getting information in an interview by developing questions that get at competency behaviors and that focus on past behavior. If you're addressing the competency of judgment, you might use a series of questions that get at past behavior, such as the following.

- What was the hardest decision you had to make in your current job?
- Tell me how you went about making it.
- What alternatives did you consider?
- What was the impact of your decision on the company? Your area?

If the person interviewed doesn't mention the specific circumstance or action he or she took, or the end result, then ask follow-up questions to get the full account. You can assess how the person behaved in the past to get a better sense of how he or she might respond in a similar situation in the future (Byham, 1996).

One of the best ways to make a great hire is to involve others in the company as part of the hiring process. Do not conduct a group interview; rather, have each person do a one-on-one interview with the candi-

TABLE 2 | **Combined Results of Interviews**

COMPETENCY	Interviewer 1	Interviewer 2	Interviewer 3
Leadership	X	X	X
Persuasiveness/ Influencing		X	X
Judgment	X		X
Innovation	X	X	
Teamwork	X		X
Planning		X	X
Integrity	X	X	

date. Group interviews are like having one big interview, and you miss the opportunity for others to contribute valuable additional information about a candidate they discover in one-on-one interviews. Assign the interviewers several of the competencies (three to six) to focus on in their interviews, with each competency having overlapping coverage. See Table 2 for an example of this.

Once the interviews are completed, have a meeting to integrate the data. The data integration portion of this process involves ranking each candidate on each competency; a simple five-point scale works well.

5—Significantly exceeds expectations (much more than acceptable for successful performance)

4—Exceeds expectations (more than acceptable)

3—Meets expectations (meets requirements for the position)

2—Approaches expectations (less than acceptable)

1—Fails to meet expectations (much less than acceptable)

During this meeting, the interviewers share notes and observations from their interviews to support their rating of a candidate on a specific competency. The goal of this meeting is to target those candidates who are qualified. Once complete, the hiring manager can then use his or her discretion to select the candidate from the qualified pool of those the team would most want to work with and who appear to be the best fit.

Herb Kelleher of Southwest Airlines often spoke of "hiring for attitude." His premise was that you can train people to develop skills, but usually not attitude. We agree that *selecting people with the right attitude and emotional skills* is a key part of hiring the right people. Some call right attitude and the corresponding emotional skills *emotional intelligence* (EI). EI involves areas such as the following:

- Self-awareness, or the ability to be conscious of your impact on others
- Assertiveness, or the ability to state how you feel and why in a nondefensive, clear way

- Empathy, or the ability to demonstrate to another that you understand how he or she feels, and why, in a variety of situations

- Impulse control, or the ability to control your anger or impatience with people and situations

These emotional factors predict how effectively people will work with each other and how successful they are in their careers and in life. Lack of emotional skills is one of the biggest reasons people in leadership roles fail.

Improving your EI is really about managing your inner response by choosing new ways to handle your inner reactions to people and situations. Mary coached a CEO we'll call Bob Smith, who had little impulse control. In meetings or even in casual interactions, he would frequently interrupt others to make his point. Worse yet, he'd unconsciously tap his finger while others spoke to mark the time before he could get his view in.

Smith initially told Mary he was baffled about why his people didn't share more with him, so her first step was to make him aware of what he was doing and the effect it was having on his team. "I honestly couldn't see how others saw me and my communications skills," Smith says. "Mary conducted confidential interviews with people who report to me. They gave her feedback on what they saw as my strengths and weaknesses, and what I could do to improve my leadership style. Then I received that information as a whole group assessment, not the opinions of individuals. I'll admit, I had a serious blind spot about the effect of my impatience with others. When I asked my wife and friends, they didn't disagree."

You can increase your EI by working on a plan to address deficits. After putting together a behavior change plan and following it diligently, Smith improved his communication skills by working on his impulse control. "As a result," Smith reports, "I have been able to build a great team who all feel they can share their insights and opinions with me. They know, too, that I am listening, not just biding my time until I can give my opinion or announce my decision."

This moves us into the area of developmental coaching for members of the work team.

Developmental Coaching

Just like all great performers, your work team members need the help of a coach to understand how they can improve and enhance their performance. Rhea Law, CEO of Fowler White Boggs Banker law firm in Florida, observes, "I personally want to make sure that the resources are there to do what we need to do to develop leadership. In that spirit we founded Fowler White University. It addresses our goal of developing others. Accepting where people are, listening to them, and coaching them are all critical factors in developing others and, I believe, constitute what it will take for us to reach our vision."

Developmental coaching can be done in-house, with supervisors and others acting as coaches or mentors from within the organization, or you can provide focused coaching using outside resources, or you can use some combination of both. As Steve Mason, CEO of Baycare Health System puts it, "I see my major accomplishments as helping others, turning caterpillars into butterflies. I look at how people solve problems to try to understand how their mind works and how they come to certain conclusions. Understanding them allows me to help and coach them better. I believe that organizations change one mind at a time."

Developmental coaching involves areas such as these:

- Identifying the strengths, weaknesses, and development needs of associates

- Applying effective strategies for developing associates

- Preparing meaningful development plans with associates and connecting them with a good succession plan

When coaching someone who reports to you, work together to identify strengths, weaknesses, and developmental needs. Let's take a brief look at some definitions of these three factors.

Characteristics of strengths

- A yearning to engage in the skill or activity

- A great deal of personal satisfaction derived from the skill or activity

- A period of rapid, almost effortless, learning to acquire the skill or perform the activity

- An insatiable desire to continue learning or perfecting the skill or activity

Characteristics of weaknesses

- A lack of aptitude for a particular skill or activity
- A dislike for doing the skill or activity
- An ability to improve on the skill or activity, though not to the point it can become a strength

Characteristics of developmental needs

- An unrealized potential for a particular skill or activity
- An enjoyment of the skill or activity, yet without the needed competence to make it truly satisfying
- An ability to improve on the skill or activity, with the ability to enhance it into a strength (Key and Capp, 2002)

Note that developmental needs are not weaknesses! An effective developmental coaching process with your employees involves building on strengths, minimizing weaknesses, and offering development opportunities to grow potential within your organization. To create a coaching culture in your company, your performance management system should assess managers on whether they coach others and prepare them for future roles in the company. Most of the CEOs we interviewed didn't start thinking about succession planning at the start; the best ones learned to build a company that fortifies and develops its bench strength through developmental coaching and honest conversations about targeting your successor.

Your Network and Support Team

As their businesses grow and the organizational complexity increases, CEOs often find that they need to work more *on* the business and less *in* the business; this is easier said than done for some CEOs, particularly if they started their businesses with a small core group of people. Their tendency is to want to maintain control of the organization, even though they know that as CEO they can no longer be as personally involved with the day-to-day operations.

As the financial and people elements of your business become more complex, you'll find yourself making decisions more frequently that involve more zeroes and feel more weighty. Due to stress, you may feel angrier than usual or that you need more time on the golf course or a long vacation to decompress. If this sounds like you, perhaps you need a personal business trainer, a coach who can guide you to training resources and help you adjust as the business grows.

When you find yourself outside of your skill set and/or comfort zone, not dealing well with the growing company and not doing anything about it, you're heading for a crash. That's why building the Right Network and support team can make all the difference. For a CEO, the support can involve an executive coach, a peer advisory board, or outside mentors.

One of the CEOs Mary has worked with, Tom Wallace, describes the importance of having a coach this way: "Tiger Woods has a swing coach . . . that's why I have used an executive coach over the years. We can all improve by having someone from the outside looking at what we are doing and challenging us. That's when we really grow. Having a coach has certainly helped me expand my businesses and be a better leader."

An executive coach can be an outside sounding board who helps you assess your and your organization's strengths and weaknesses. By drafting a plan to address areas such as your changing role as the organization grows or a blind spot that keeps you from being more successful as a leader, you can learn to be more strategic and work more on your company and making your vision a reality.

Similarly, a CEO peer advisory board, composed of people from *outside* your organization, can help immensely with that lonely-at-the-top feeling that plagues many CEOs in need of an impartial look at their company. Such executive forums with other smart CEOs from diverse businesses will allow you to tap into the collective intelligence and experience of the group. Many CEOs report when meeting with their advisory board that they finally get the no-holds-barred feedback they need from peers who have no vested interest in what decision the CEO bringing the issue to the group might make.

Many CEOs in our study found lifelong friends among the CEOs gathered at a forum; they continue to talk to one another about business problems, life balance, and a host of other shared opportunities and challenges. For many participating in a forum or advisory group, this is the first real opportunity to develop what we like to call professional intimacy with others. Mary has facilitated CEO forums for ten years and has found that many of the CEOs continue to participate together over long periods of time, or at least maintain a network that serves as a resource and support. She has found that CEO peers are a critical part of the right network in times of stress, such as going through a break-up of a business partnership or a marriage, as well as for information on everything from good venture capitalists to attorneys with certain specialties.

Your Home Team

Another key predictor of success in your business and personal life is whom you choose as a life partner. Here are a few interesting observations that came out of our research.

- Over 80 percent of our CEO group is married.
- Over 75 percent of those who are married rate their marriages as at least an 8, on a 1-to-10 scale measuring satisfaction with the partnership.

- About 70 percent of the top CEOs are still married to the same person they were married to when they became an executive.

- Most of the CEOs have had the usual ups and downs of marriage, but when the chips were down with their business or family life, these couples supported each other well and came out of the crisis generally stronger.

Gene Corrigan, former CEO of the Atlantic Coast Conference, referred to in an earlier chapter, relied heavily on his wife, Lena, as he was traveling a lot in the early days of his career and she was raising their seven children. When he could, he made time to be home and encouraged her to get away with friends, which helped him to bond with his kids and gave her much-needed mental health breaks. When times got tough with his career or with family problems, they always respected each other's opinion and looked for ways to support the other. "Gene has a great ability to make me feel listened to," says Lena. "I felt like we always have been a team in everything and have faced both tragedy and triumph together."

When things got tough on the home front, the majority of the top CEOs we interviewed had some form of counseling and some participated in pre- or postmarital workshops that helped them examine their shared values and beliefs, as well as taught them ways to communicate more effectively with each other. Here is some of the advice these CEOs offered.

- Invest the same amount of time and energy in reconnecting to your partner, talking and listening, and being empathetic that you would give to your largest customer.
- Go to marital health workshops periodically.
- Consider a marriage counselor; get over any prejudices you may have about therapy.
- Try to rekindle the fire; build on shared experiences.

Some of the CEOs disliked the idea that their relationships might be "broken" and need to be "fixed" by a therapist. Consider instead *wellness tune-ups* at regular intervals, usually monthly or quarterly, when things are going pretty well. If you have these resources in place early and use them effectively, they can help you be proactive in dealing not only with challenges at work, but also in your marriage, with your children, and with other significant relationships in your life.

Networking for the Right People

Whether you're looking for someone to join your work, support, or home team, networking can help you find the right people. In fact, the Right Network can assist you in finding the Right People (and avoid the wrong ones). The really successful networkers in our group found that one friend often led to making friends with others in that person's network and so on, to the point that the network took on a life of its own, constrained only by the executive's ability to connect and have meaningful relationships with a geometrically growing group of friends and colleagues.

Our CEOs also told us stories of how they found their marriage partner, business partner, banker, and other resources that served as great supports through the informal networks they developed. Usually the network grew as the CEO took the initiative to participate in community and church activities; professional, trade, or industry associations; and peer advisory boards. Even if you are not an especially great networker, befriending someone who is can often lead to many new contacts and relationships.

David Bruce, founder and former head of an engineering company, started networking out of college and found the contacts he made to be invaluable in figuring out the business he wanted to run someday, lining up early customers, and observing the mistakes of his fraternity brothers on what not to do when starting your own business. "I made a commitment to be part of Rotary, went to the Chamber of Commerce lunches, became part of a CEO roundtable group, and joined a variety of organizations. An early mentor and an executive coach helped me understand the power of the network. Rather than overtly try to sell to people I met as my network developed, I built long-term relationships that helped me every step of the way.

"You could almost say I developed into a master networker, but anti-salesman. I avoided marrying the wrong woman when network peers helped me understand what a bad match we were. I then met my current wife and true love through the network when friends who knew each of us arranged a date. I have been a better father by seeking out people in my network who have obviously done a good job of raising their kids and have sought their advice often. My wife has done the same thing to help her be a better mother and to enhance her career. Networking was also a key component in the twenty-five-year success of my company. I even sold it to someone I had developed a friendship with in my network fifteen years before. As I think back, I'm not sure I could have accomplished half of what I have personally and professionally and dealt with all the hard times without having invested so much in my network."

Obviously, a big plus of networking is the accessibility of better resources to find people for your Right Team. Many successful CEOs won't even consider someone for a senior position unless they have personally observed the candidate in action or talked extensively with people they trust who have worked with the candidate. Many in our CEO group use their networks to:

- Circulate career openings
- Evaluate candidates using extended networking with friends and colleagues
- Learn of talented people they may want to get to know even before they have a specific job slot for that person

- Find like-minded people to associate with on a day-to-day basis
- Get feedback on important business decisions before enacting them
- Meet people to interact with on a more comfortable and more personal level

Top CEOs are always on the lookout for people to add to their team. Al Bodford uses his network to find the best people. He asks people within his network what potential candidates' work and personal ethics are and observes candidates' behavior in competing companies, at industry association meetings, and through the eyes of his team. This gives him a good idea of how his company's mission-vision-values will line up with the way his candidate does business. "This is the best system I know of to find and hire good people," says Bodford. "I've tried other methods and occasionally find a gem among the hundreds of resumes we receive, but direct experience with someone who knows the candidate has helped me avoid the jokers and find the aces."

Networking for Personal Success

Interestingly, some of the latest aging studies conclude that one of the top predictors of living long and well is your social network, particularly if it relieves stress in your life. A well-established network can help you transition into retirement and will become a support group for you after your business is sold. We know that stress can be a killer. Successful CEOs we have worked with adapted well to stress during their work life, but the ones who really shined after they left their business had a healthy social network.

A MacArthur Foundation study that evaluated 4,000 older people from Massachusetts, North Carolina, and Connecticut focused on the one-third of the group who had the highest mental and physical function at the outset. Researchers then followed up with them three and eight years into the study. A high frequency of emotional support, which included meeting and interacting well with family and friends, was a powerful predictor of who in the group ended up improving their mental and physical state. Having good friends and family in your life increases the likelihood that you will get out more, keep moving, and actually *improve* with age.

Win Dermody, a former packaging company owner, believes that networking at multiple levels was one of his keys to success. Over the years, Dermody served as a prominent local government official, Chamber board president, and member of a state leadership organization; and he took part in a host of other pursuits that he enjoyed, met friends, and showcased his skills and abilities to help each become more successful. As he says, "My network of friends and business colleagues stretches coast–to-coast. Many helped me in business without my even asking for their help. Some became mentors and guided me in my journey to become a better husband and father. Today, part of my successful retirement is due in large part to this wonderful network that started over forty years ago."

Networking for the Next Generation

Teach the next generation how to network: your children's network may extend around the world, and their ability to connect and stay connected may be a key differentiator in their future success and resilience in response to the massive changes that are ahead.

Have you thought about your children's current network and what they are learning from it, good or bad? In our wired world, they are probably networking with good people and not-so-good people every day. Whether choosing someone to date, potential business associates, their career path, or their investment strategy, they need best practices from their wiser elders more than ever.

Dennis has used youth coaches for his clients' children and grandchildren. These coaches can help focus young people on their own Right Road, deal with issues in high school and college or beyond that they are not comfortable sharing with their parents, and provide an additional network that can help them succeed and define their own meaning of significance.

None of the CEOs we interviewed or have worked with who have reported fulfilling careers and lives perceive that they've done it alone. Right People in every aspect and stage of your life can make the difference between struggle and failure or success and significance.

Assess the right people in your life—your work team, your network and support team, and your home team.

Remember **past behavior speaks volumes about future behavior.** This principle can help you improve all hiring and partnering decisions.

Resist the urge to get someone in place fast if you aren't sure of their skill set or the fit.

Build a **systematic selection and hiring process** and stick to it.

Make coaching a requirement for everyone in a leadership role in your organization and set up consequences if they do it well or if they don't.

•

Join a peer advisory board and use the forum as an opportunity to work through your top business issues and to network.

•

Make time for your friends and family. If necessary, schedule time with them in your planner. They are your biggest supporters and need you as much as your business does.

•

Make time to network with others you respect **who may be ahead of you in a key area(s).** Think of it like planning— you have an initial time investment up front, but the return on your investment is priceless.

•

Consider ways to coach and find coaches for your children and grandchildren. Help them surround themselves with strong network resources.

CHAPTER
6

THE RIGHT RESILIENCY

Change continues to accelerate, and keeping pace is challenging. Entrepreneurial organizations are often more agile than their larger competitors and have used that competency as their competitive advantage. The best closely held businesses have a history of being able to adapt to changing market forces faster than larger, more bureaucratic, organizations. Most businesspeople know that if you can serve the customer faster, better, and cheaper, *and* make a profit, you're on to something. Agility, then, is the ability to adjust and thrive in response to ongoing or continuous change.

In contrast, *resiliency* is the ability to handle abrupt or discontinuous change. Such change involves unexpected shocks that may threaten survival, such as terrorist attacks, mass credit card theft from a company Web site, a hurricane or tsunami, or losing a business partner, as Joe did. One characteristic that separates the best CEOs from the rest is their resiliency, or mental toughness, in a crisis.

A true story that exemplifies resiliency, and that has become a classic in some circles, is what happened when Malden Mills burned (Manz et al. 2001). Mill owner Aaron Feuerstein and his family went out to celebrate his seventieth birthday. That's when the call came. His clothing business went up in flames. Feuerstein immediately went to the work site. The firemen were able to save a portion of the complex, but not nearly enough for the business to stay operational. That evening, Feuerstein made a tough call. He would keep his employees on the payroll while the mill was being rebuilt with the contingency that they would have to perform at record levels to make the numbers work.

The workers knew how easy it would be for Feuerstein to take his production off-shore and leave them in the lurch. Their dedication and resiliency, alongside Feuerstein's, helped the business survive. The grateful workforce temporarily accepted less pay and broke all past production records.

Dennis had the opportunity to meet Feuerstein while working on a business planning project for a brand extension line of clothes using Polartec® fabrics. Feuerstein told Dennis that his people were one of his greatest resources for resiliency, a comment we have heard often in our interviews with top CEOs.

In contrast, the airline industry has had a tough time recovering after 9/11. One exception is Southwest Airlines, which doesn't use the same business model of strong dependence on a larger and more expensive system of booking customers, maintaining equipment, and providing other services.

Some companies, like the bond trading firm Cantor Fitzgerald, lost most of its employees housed in the World Trade Center. Yet they survived and now thrive in their niche.

What separates the leaders and organizations who handle disruptive change well from those who don't? Many factors come into play (McCann 2004); several are worth mentioning and were confirmed in our interviews with CEOs who were faced with the crisis of disruptive change.

1. Get mentally tough and build resiliency on an ongoing basis.

2. Be an organization that can learn and relearn from experiences, so you can reinvent your company when and as necessary.

3. Plan for crises and anticipate what might happen so you can recover from abrupt change.

Mental Toughness

The concept of "mental toughness" came out of sports psychology, where innovators like James Loehr (1993) noticed that some athletes were able to use their energy wisely and efficiently, while others were not. The difference between good performance and great performance has everything to do with what you tell yourself and visualize before, during, and after you perform. Building mental toughness involves noticing physiological changes in your body, as well as noticing what you say to yourself while you're performing or acting in a crisis. Observing physical and mental patterns allows you to adjust or change them when what you are doing depletes your resiliency (Loehr and Schwartz, 2003).

Pioneer in stress research Hans Selye differentiated between external "stress" and the internal "strain" that stress causes. He noted three stress stages: *alarm* (fight-or-flight response); *resistance* (dealing with the challenge); and *exhaustion* (when mental and physiological resources are depleted).

People who haven't honed their resiliency system may stay in the fight-or-flight phase too long when confronted with a stressful situation. Their blood pressure may remain elevated, heart rate may increase, and a host of other physiological responses may kick in. Cardiologists and heart disease specialists believe that staying in a continuing state of stress creates greater risk of heart attacks, strokes, bleeding ulcers, and cancer.

Resilient people manage to build their mental toughness to perform under stress and to move through the stages of stress. They then take the time to replenish so they can deal with new challenges refreshed. Stress is an inevitable part of life. Learning how to regulate its impact on you and your organization is the key to staying resilient. We all need some stress in our lives to grow; however, we must also learn how to balance our alarm and resistance phases with rest and relaxation during the exhaustion phase. Usually a person's or company's inability to allow for essential downtime for recuperation leads to *dis*tress.

You can build resiliency through the experience of handling smaller crises; they can help you prepare for a big crisis. Peter Heineman, former "Smoked Salmon King of New York," relates how challenging problems prepared him, bit by bit, for the big one when his business burned to the ground in a January snowstorm. "You just don't realize early on how every little problem you handle as a CEO helps you deal with the next one better," he says. "All the early problems I dealt with helped me deal with the really big stuff. I also let strangers help along the way, including the building inspector who bent a lot of rules to help me get back on my feet. When you deal with the worst and get past the panic and being exhausted, you develop a calmness so that you can handle just about anything the world throws at you."

During crises in their business and home lives, resilient leaders find healthy ways to deal with their feelings, even when the circumstances are blatantly unfair. Whether dealing with a loved one's breast cancer just when everything else was starting to click, or losing funding at a crucial time in your work or business, your inner strength and creative tools can be invaluable.

Peter Duke is the former CEO of Smartwool, a company he recently sold. His story is classic entrepreneur, with a path to success that would have been hard to plan in advance. A gifted athlete, Duke dreamed of becoming a professional baseball player, and in the eleventh grade he went to a tryout for the New York Yankees. But his parents had other plans, mainly that he come into the family beer distributorship. He started out at the University of Miami before the military draft changed his plans again. After leaving the military and joining the family business, he discovered that he loved skiing in New England and left the "sure thing" to become a ski instructor. He later became a member of the Professional Ski Instructors Association Alpine Team and represented the 9th Interski Team for the USA in Garmisch, Germany.

When Duke was in his late thirties, he and his wife started making ski hats and apparel. They were sure they were in their area of passion, but it took them ten years, with many challenges, to develop Smartwool, which is now a major brand in the ski and outdoor industry. Duke recalls that just as they were starting out, his wife developed breast cancer. As she battled for her life, the entire family focused on supporting her treatment and recovery. Their two boys took up the challenge and helped out more at home as Duke honored his wife's wishes and stayed focused on the business launch. "My path to success was anything but a straight arrow," says Duke. "I'm a twenty-year, up-and-down and all-over-the-mountain overnight success!"

One of the ways to develop inner strength is to notice your "self-talk" or what you might be saying to yourself during a trying time. Saying things such as "this will never work" or "I always get the short end of the stick" will only deplete your stamina. Observing your internal conversations and learning to consciously adjust your thinking builds resilience. Change your pattern by affirming that "this can work" or "we are growing stronger through this challenge."

Ironically, being your own boss, which many view as being *more* stressful, can actually be *less* stressful because business owners often feel they are more in control. If you're working for someone else, especially for a large company, you may feel helpless to control the future, as if you're subject to the whims of people you don't necessarily trust or respect. But in truth it's all about your perception of the situations and events that come into your life. Whether you run your own company or work for someone else, seeing problems as challenges, so that working on them becomes energizing, not depleting, can build resiliency.

Several of the CEOs we interviewed developed an attitude of resilience that has helped them build stamina for future challenges. Win Dermody had been fired as the general manager of a privately held packaging company for personal reasons of the CEO that had little to do with Dermody's performance. Dermody knew the business, loved it, and wanted to control his own destiny going forward. The work was purposeful for him. So, after losing his job, he started his own packaging business. The idea of not having a boss making arbitrary decisions that affected his life appealed to him. Driven by focused anger and a desire to create something special, Dermody's vision statement became "Be the compelling choice for customers, with great packaging, fair prices, and great customer service."

Dermody combined Right Focus with the Right People and Right Execution. Top talent in his industry gravitated to his positive attitude and keen intellect. He worked long hours and set a pace that inspired his team. As a result, competitors simply couldn't keep up with him. Three years later, as his former boss declared bankruptcy, his company was on the way to being one of the largest private packaging companies in the state. This was an important part of Right Focus and is critical to Right Resiliency.

Your Preferred Future

A key factor in developing mental resiliency, and also something that stood out in interviewing CEOs, is the power of visualization. CEO of Bromley Companies Bill Haines explains, "I'm five to ten years in the future every day. I involve someone else in dealing with today, and I stay in the future. I picture what I'd like to see happen; however, I don't see the future as only the way I'd want to see it. I work hard at honestly attempting to assess and reassess what's occurring on a daily basis."

Visualization is significantly correlated with high performance in athletics and in other areas of life, such as in reaching business and personal goals. Visualization is the ability to picture vividly and specifically your preferred future. What Haines unknowingly described is a process that Robert Fritz has researched and written about in his best-selling book, *The Path of Least Resistance.* In it, Fritz outlines a visualization process in which you picture your desired future or goal, and then you picture it juxtaposed against the current reality. The "structural tension" from this mental comparison propels you to seek resolution, and you are more likely to achieve your desired goal or end state as a result.

Years ago, Mary was in no position to own her dream car, a Jaguar, when she started picturing herself driving a champagne-colored XJ6 Vanden Plas. For weeks on end she'd look at a picture of it that she kept on the refrigerator. She'd picture herself driving the car and enjoying the sights and sounds. She allowed herself to feel the discrepancy between driving her aging Toyota and her dream car. Within a month and a half, after reading the classifieds every day, Mary saw her future car described to a T. The ad started "Must sell my dream car." The owner and her husband were leaving for a two-year assignment in Europe. The seller didn't want just anyone to buy her dream car. She actually sold it to Mary at a discount because she could see her own enthusiasm for the car in Mary's eyes.

On a business level, the majority of our CEOs commented that if it were their last day on the job and they were addressing the organization on what they accomplished together, it would be the joint effort to fulfill the mission and reach a vision or significant goal together. Reaching a joint goal involves the collective minds and hearts of those committed to the goal uniting in seeing their preferred reality as if it existed in the present. At the same time, an honest assessment of the gap between where you are now and where you want to be is essential. You can reinforce the attainment of your vision by displaying relevant symbols and pictures, telling descriptive stories of how people are working toward the vision, and providing specific data to track progress.

Peter Heineman's smoked salmon business had just set a record in revenues and profits when it burned to the ground. His mental toughness, ability to visualize a better future, and team of loyal employees helped him set a record profit in the next three months and a record for the same year. When he won the Ernst & Young Entrepreneur of the Year award years later, one reason the judges cited was Heineman's uncommon ability to rebound so quickly from a disaster that would have spelled doom for many businesses. Heineman sums it up, "I learned from my father that being a shlump of any kind was unacceptable. Then I successfully worked with a lot of unbelievably tough customers when I was building my business. You just don't realize how all those character-building problems you figure out the answers to early on will come back to help you later in life. My dream of building a successful business was stronger than any disaster."

Attention to Your Body's Needs

Diet and exercise, along with humor, are important ingredients in building resiliency. Our eating habits can have a big effect on our emotional state. For example, we are more likely to get cranky or be argumentative if our blood sugar is low. Nutritious meals that energize us coupled with regular aerobic and anaerobic exercise will give us the stamina to perform at high levels. Having a strong body and mind, together with building in life-balancing relaxation, bolsters personal resiliency. Kindermusik International's Michael Dougherty puts it this way: "Before I ran my own company, I didn't always take the time off I needed to be with my family and recharge my batteries. Now I find some way every day and every week to do good, healthy things for my body and my mind. I can tell my coping abilities are better as a result."

Humor can ease tension and allows us and others around us to take a mental relaxation break. Laughter also helps us to breathe deeper, which allows more oxygen to circulate in our bloodstream. Many outstanding companies have learned how to use humor and fun to take the edge off the stress from exerting energy on projects and meeting daunting deadlines. Such companies encourage bringing humor into the workplace by joking, having silly contests, or telling humorous stories about each other. Like people, organizations need to take mental relaxation breaks to induce needed downtime for replenishing energy.

One of the CEOs we interviewed runs a worldwide learning center that does leadership workshops. He believes that "childlike curiosity," which includes having fun, is a key to the early success of entrepreneurs and to their ability to deal with change. He now teaches Fortune 500 companies how to "think creatively like an entrepreneur" and is an advisor to several "intra-preneurial subsidiaries," the new way that big companies are trying to create the feel and adaptability of more agile and resilient entrepreneurial companies.

The Learning Organization

In his book *The Fifth Discipline,* Peter Senge was among the first to bring forth the idea and importance of an organization becoming a "learning organization," or an open system that continues to learn from its experiences and from the expertise of people within and outside the company. To be a learning organization, you must see your company as a system that has many interconnections within and outside itself.

Learning from the past and capitalizing on the collective intelligence of your organization allows you to reinvent your company after a crisis if necessary. One of the CEOs we interviewed lost everything due to a change in interest rates. He was able to rebuild his company using a different approach to his market and leveraging his past, learning to create with others from his old organization a new company that was more streamlined, profitable, and better positioned for the changing market in the future. Sometimes, old structures no longer serve you, and it isn't until we face a crisis that we learn to think creatively, as if we were drawing the organization on a new sheet of paper.

View your business as a system with many interdependencies, such as the interactions between departments, with vendors, and with outsourcing partners. Noticing how and to whom you are connected helps you understand where you are exposed and dependent; knowing where your organization fits into a broader system can help you anticipate where you need to grow or change and where you might be vulnerable if there were a crisis or disruptive change of some kind. Systems thinking can also assist you in understanding how future trends may affect you because you aren't just seeing the company in isolation or only in relationship to your customers. When you take a big-picture view of all the interrelationships, you can learn more about what other stakeholders see in the future.

In doing so, many of the top CEOs we interviewed have been studying various megatrends. One conclusion is that the rate of change we will see in the next twenty years will eclipse that of the past twenty, causing anxiety, stress, and anger at unprecedented levels, right along with huge opportunities to grow individually and to prosper in business and in life. Opportunities and threats are nothing new to many entrepreneurs. However, if this change happens so fast that it upsets the balance of the supply chain, your company employees, community organizations you serve, and perhaps even your family and friends, you may find yourself needing resiliency and agility skills at a higher level than ever before.

Just because your company is resilient and successful doesn't mean that all your upstream and downstream vendors, partners, and suppliers are equally resilient. A number of the CEOs we interviewed now grade their entire supply chain based on factors such as their faith in each link's leaders, financial strength, history of working through tough times with the company, relationship of key employees in the link with their own, and how they rank on the food chain within this system. If our interdependencies are broad, we are more likely to be exposed to greater risk if some unexpected change occurs. Carrying on business as usual isn't possible if our stakeholders aren't resilient.

Systems at Home Too

Examining the system of interdependencies applies to your personal life as well. Having a strong social network is a key to bouncing back from setbacks, whether we're talking about health, money, or family issues. Who you, your life partner, and children associate with every day can affect your (and their) outlook on the world, providing support and growth or allowing problems to creep into an otherwise healthy environment.

One CEO we interviewed agonized over a friend of his wife's who was constantly in some crisis situation or getting into trouble with the law, mutual friends, or others in their social network. The CEO's wife slowly lost confidence in her own ability to handle crises, since anything she did to help her friend seemed to have no positive effect. When they noticed how invested their mother was in rescuing her friend, the couple's children began to mimic the behavior of the friend and got caught shoplifting. This brush with the law was the last straw. It's hard to tell someone you love that she needs to "fire" a friend, but that became the only solution. Now this couple's life includes only friends who are healthy in body, mind, and spirit, and, as parents, they are modeling this healthy system for their children.

The real danger is that sometimes those people in your network who are pulling your level of resiliency down aren't easy to spot. Notice who drains your energy and who refills it. Make a conscious decision about who you want to affiliate with and make sure it's a mutually supportive relationship.

Distance in Observing

One of the hallmarks of a resilient leader is the ability to go into a third-party observer mode and view the current situation from a detached and more objective perspective. When you can disengage from the emotion of the situation and see a variety of perspectives, you open yourself to finding a creative alternative to a challenge in your business or life. "I've always dealt with adversity and bounced back better than my peers due in part to my playful child always being just beneath the surface," says Frank Pope, a partner in an investment bank in California who has bounced back from multiple shocks to his business and family that could have put him out of action. "I look at problems in a detached way with a curiosity about what would happen if I turned the problem around like a prism. Sometimes those around me wonder when I laugh at the amusing parts of a crisis, but they know its part of my coping mechanism."

Not all of the CEOs we interviewed feel as capable of looking at a challenge creatively. To compensate, they build a team around them that complements them and makes up for their blind spot. As one of our CEOs noted, "Creativity has always been my biggest challenge. I can analyze and execute with the best of them, but I can't always be as creative as others on my team or as my wife, who is involved in the business. It's been good for me to be open to what others think when I'm faced with adversity. It seems that the slower I am to dismiss ideas, the more good ideas keep flowing. Sometimes the best idea comes from looking at the problem from a completely different angle, often not my own."

Crisis Planning and Anticipating Abrupt Change

Many of the CEOs we interviewed have disaster plans in place in the event of fire, hurricanes, and other natural catastrophes. Some put the crisis plan into place only after a disaster almost wiped them out. Most of the top CEOs in our study went beyond the typical disaster plan and have contingencies for a number of occurrences, even if they can't pinpoint what would cause the problem in the first place. One example is communication via cell phones.

After 9/11, cell lines were jammed for hours in New York City and around the country. Many companies realized that this was a weak link when it came to disaster communication. In response, they invested in satellite phones, dedicated telecom lines, and other technology to deal with a problem that could result from any number of calamities.

We have already discussed examining the supply chain weaknesses. Have you run "fire drills" in which different suppliers are assumed to lose capacity for some reason? Figuring out in advance what the options are and who the best alternate supply chain players would be to turn to quickly is a valuable exercise. Some CEOs are currently running bird flu what-if scenarios so they can figure out how to keep their business running if 50 percent of their employees aren't able to show up for work, even though some might be able to work from home. You may not be able to figure out foolproof ways to avoid the negative effects of catastrophes, but the discipline of asking "what if" will help you and your team build better resiliency skills to deal with crises.

This reminds us of the story of the two guys camping in the woods who are confronted with a bear. One starts putting on his tennis shoes. His friend says, "You're crazy. You can't outrun that bear." His friend replies, "I don't need to outrun the bear. I just need to outrun you!" Most of your business competitors are probably reactive, able to deal only with the crises at hand; even a little edge may be just what you need to survive and prosper after the next actual disaster occurs.

In the Right Planning chapter, we discussed some of the powerful uses of scenario learning to help you better visualize and prepare for an uncertain future. Using these techniques to help your family plan ahead can provide a great framework for better resiliency in the face of crises. Families that ricochet from eating lobster in good times to hot dogs in tough times may feel high anxiety, particularly in the earlier stages of building the business when cash flow isn't plentiful or predictable. If you have a good plan in place that helps smooth out spending and other decisions to minimize severe ups and downs, you'll experience a greater feeling of control, which leads to better resiliency when really tough times come along.

Helping Your Kids Become Resilient

Have you ever wondered why the children and grandchildren of successful people seem to turn out less and less successful? "I see my CEO friends trying to keep their kids from having the same problems they had," says Peter Duke, former CEO of Smartwool. "I guess it's natural for us all to want our kids to have a better life, but protecting them from change and crisis has the opposite effect. It's no wonder these kids hit this 'ever-changing at breakneck speed' world and go into complete shock or denial."

Kids need to continually learn life's tough lessons, especially as the family's standard of living increases and the business becomes less risky. As we all know, if you say one thing and do another, children won't respect you as a teacher. Part of helping your children be resilient is to help them be better decision makers in all areas of their life.

One example is to separate the must-have "necessities" from the nice-to-have "luxuries." A TV commercial for an online stock trading firm shows a father and daughter talking about designer jeans. The daughter makes the jeans look like a "must have" because all the kids have them—the pressure from commercial ads and peers is relentless. Dad decides to research the company that makes the jeans, buys a hundred shares, and thanks his daughter for the "opportunity." This ad shows the father caving at the end and buying his daughter the jeans. The message is if you whine long enough and loud enough, you'll get what you want. But if you give in, your chances of raising an independent adult are greatly reduced, which will almost ensure that your child will get Ds and Fs in "life resiliency" and be boomeranging back into your life every time things get tough.

"I found opportunities for the kids to stretch themselves and confront change," says Barbara Collie, who supported her husband, Joe, through many long, tough years building Southchem, his chemical distribution business. She continues, "Our parenting approach was to give our children the same gift we had had when we were young—the ability to be challenged, tough it out, and learn about the hard knocks of the world. They had to work for everything, even when they complained that their friends were being given the world on a silver platter. The biggest challenge of being successful is to avoid ruining the values and ethics of your family." Teach your kids to stretch and problem solve, for example, through attending youth leadership programs and working for their luxury items. Do the same for your grandchildren.

It comes down to this: when you have honed your resiliency skills by getting mentally tough, learning and relearning as an organization and family, seeing the preferred future, and preparing for crises, you can recognize a situation for what it is and respond appropriately. As you face down tough challenges and manage to prosper, you come to believe that you can handle future challenges similarly. You might actually look forward to confronting new challenges and to solving difficult situations creatively.

•

Change is constant. **Being resilient and agile** is essential to creating success and significance in your life.

•

Get mentally tough and build resiliency on an ongoing basis.

- Notice what you say to yourself and change your self-talk if it's negative.

- Continually visualize your preferred outcome.

- Eat right and exercise frequently.

- Use humor; it takes the edge off and can help you be more creative in a challenging situation.

•

Be an organization that keeps learning from experiences.

- See your business and your life as a system of inter-connections.

- Preserve best practices from your past and adopt good ideas from others.

- Anticipate future trends and brainstorm how to deal with the challenges and opportunities they bring.

- Detach yourself from the crisis and see it from a third-person observer perspective.

- Plan for crises and anticipate what might happen so you can recover from abrupt change.

- Model and teach others, including your children, to be resilient.

PART THREE

EXECUTION

THE RIGHT EXECUTION

You've found your Right Road, determined the Right Focus, and made the Right Plan. You've also focused on finding and developing the Right People on your team— at work, at home, and in your network. Now it's time to go the distance. Perhaps the most difficult and yet most rewarding area of concentration is the next one, executing with excellence, or what we call Right Execution.

"Execution is one of the key things I focused on every day because I could see instant feedback through results," says Peter Heineman, the former Salmon King of New York. "As my focus became more honed, my people became more experienced, and my network gained power; it felt like momentum happened almost on its own. But we still had to make it happen every day."

The Right Execution Principles

After his visit with Darrell, the CEO mentor from the future, Joe realized how his company had become less and less effective at executing. He didn't have the first two priorities right—Focus and People—but he compensated early on by working hard and executing well. As Joe's company grew, he didn't know how to keep this up, and then the shortcomings of not having a plan and not having all the right people caught up with him. The CEOs we interviewed echoed this problem. Some things became easier as they grew, such as the owner not having to wear quite as many hats, but most day-to-day activities became more difficult as decisions were required constantly and also had more zeroes attached to them.

Execution fails for a variety of reasons. One of the most common is not helping employees connect with the company's overall direction and helping them see where their efforts tie into something larger. Consider these alarming statistics from *Harris Interactive,* cited by Stephen Covey (2004).

- Only 15 percent of people in organizations can identify the most important goals or top priorities

- Only 19 percent feel passionate about the organization's goals

- Of those working on priority goals, approximately 49 percent of their time is focused on these goals

- Some 51 percent of people in organizations don't understand what they personally can do to meet the goals being communicated

We have found several key reasons for the failure of execution; these dovetail with the *Harris Interactive*'s findings above.

- Leaders lack an integrated focus and strategy or have not translated the strategy into what others need to work on effectively.
- Accountability systems either are not in place or are incomplete.
- Capabilities do not exist in the organization to execute the strategy.

In turn, the best performing companies consistently do the following.

- *The leaders model the behaviors they expect and make communicating the vision and strategy a priority.*

The most innovative CEOs we've interviewed and worked with communicate clearly and often the direction the organization is going in; this includes talking about the vision, goals, strategy, and values using examples and stories so that people understand at fundamental levels. One of the CEOs we interviewed, Harry Teasley, a longtime senior executive with the Coca-Cola Company, states, "I believe one of the gifts I've given people is clarity. I have always communicated our entire strategy to prepare my people to do well and understand why what they are doing is important."

Even more critical is the CEO's role in modeling expectations. Teasley recalls a time when, as the new managing director of an English Coca-Cola bottling operation, he led through example and set the stage for effective execution. As he explains,

> At a weekly meeting of my directors (vice presidents), I was informed that an hourly warehouse employee had been fired for stealing two cases of company products. Yet all of the directors took free product home on a regular basis, a long-standing practice sanctioned by my predecessor. What's more, they asked the warehouse employees to carry the product to their cars. I couldn't help but see the ethical, leadership, and modeling issues of firing a low-wage warehouse worker for an activity that high-salary executives did with impunity. The situation was made even more complicated by the long-standing class divisions in England and the fact that I was both new to the position and an American in a foreign culture.
>
> I thought about issuing a formal policy statement ending the practice of directors taking free product, or calling a meeting to discuss the issue, but believed both alternatives had the potential of major unintended consequences among the directors.
>
> At noon the next day, I went to the company store, where employees could purchase product at a substantial discount, and stood in line. Surprised to see me, the employees offered to let me go to the front of the line but I refused. When my turn came, I ordered two cases of product and paid for it with a sockful of change I'd brought to work for that purpose. Despite

offers to help me, I carried the product to the car myself.

By three that afternoon, it seemed every employee in the United Kingdom had heard the story. I never had a single word or discussion with any of the directors, but the free-goods practice came to an immediate end, as did the stealing by plant and warehouse workers. Leading by example is essential to executing well. By all measures our operation became successful.

As an old story goes, a very effective CEO was asked his secret to creating a highly successful and significant organization, in that it contributed to others and the community far beyond the company's financial success. The CEO replied, "That's simple. I get up and communicate the vision; then the next day, I communicate the vision; then for each day after, I communicate the vision."

One thing many of our CEOs told us is that, to their initial amazement, you can't over-communicate the vision and how the initiatives being taken fit under it. Michael Dougherty of Kindermusik International says, "Communicating our vision and how we plan to execute on it, or what I call our 'execution messages,' is always a challenge. We over-communicate all the time to make sure our messages are sticking. All of our team members are busy at work and lead busy lives at home, so it's easy for our execution drivers to get lost in the daily grind. So we talk about the vision and what drives it weekly and sometimes daily at meetings. We post them on boards internally. Our team knows exactly what the program is at all times!"

- *The leaders see execution as a major job, and accountability is essential to it; performance expectations and measures are clear and tracked, providing ongoing feedback.*

Right Execution involves aligning your actions with your plan and following through to achieve results. For many organizations, it's the hardest thing to do well because getting everyone to understand the plan, their part in it, and how to implement on time and within budget *together* takes clarity, skill, and commitment. People need to be clear and excited about the direction as well as willing to take ownership for the desired results and behaviors expected. Unless people get relevant feedback on measured results, your ability to execute effectively is compromised.

In an interview with Dave Dunkel, CEO of KForce, he described his success formula this way: "Our major accomplishments are really about attracting and retaining a talented team of people, planning, and focusing on results, processes, systems, and implementation with timelines and metrics. By creating a culture of accountability for the right things, we are fulfilling our vision of being the most respected staffing firm to those we serve."

Break your plan down into broad-based goals that set a direction, such as the goal of "attracting and retaining top talent." Next, identify specific observable, measurable, or verifiable objectives that further define your goals, and assign ownership and accountability, such as "developing a succession planning process and mapping out a plan for the organization by the end of this year." Once you establish objectives for individuals and teams, you can develop action plans so you can implement steps to reach the objectives and ultimately the goals set. Goals tend to be two to five years out, while objectives may be more short term or simply ongoing.

You build an implementation plan by including those who do the work when mapping out the action steps to get there. As Darrell, the CEO from the future, advised Joe, *involve all key stakeholders in your implementation plan and create a culture that places a priority on executing with excellence.* The old top-down, authoritative style worked for some CEOs in their early days, but as their company and the world changed, they found it worked better to involve as many people as possible in the planning process. Whether you are creating a plan, fixing a broken plan, or updating a successful plan, include as many of the people who execute the plan daily as you can. Some high-performing organizations involve their customers, vendors, and strategic partners in the implementation planning process as well. Get key stakeholder input, make them feel heard, and act on good ideas that fit your direction and strategy.

"I have CEO friends who prefer their people at their desks helping customers, or on planes going to sell product," says Blanche Dubois, CEO of a design-build firm in Florida. "They think this is getting maximum productivity out of their people. In my book, it's maximum stupidity. The right hand doesn't know what the left hand is doing. Getting employees off-site, sharpening their axes, keeping them fresh, and having them feel like they're part of planning their own futures: now, that's what I'm talking about!"

Sometimes the action steps require changing the workflow or the design of how things get done. When you can accomplish these changes in real time, people feel energized because their observations and ideas count. Creating a culture that executes with excellence involves acting with a sense of urgency, particularly if the actions recommended can make a difference and clearly don't need a lot of deliberation. Empowering others to make decisions is an essential building block to creating ownership; unless the majority of employees feel that their expertise and skills are valued, mediocrity sets in. Here's how one of our CEOs, Leo Bontempo, former president of Syngenta, explained it.

My staff and every employee down to the janitor always had a good working knowledge of our execution priorities and, maybe more important, a say in how things got done. Our top execution areas for each person were even posted on their office doors with the legend, "If you can't help me with one of these areas, think twice before coming in!" Top to bottom, bottom to top, whatever you call it, it's getting everyone involved and enthusiastic around making it happen the right way every single day.

It's great to have a comprehensive plan, but if you don't communicate it well, you often fail. We have worked with a lot of leadership teams to develop plans in a retreat setting; when the participants return to the office, they often assume that others in the organization will somehow understand what needs to be done

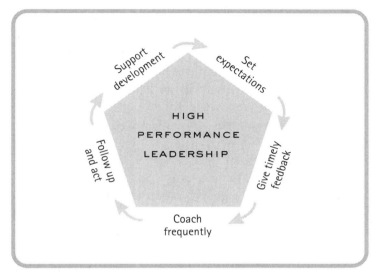

Figure 2 High Performance Leadership Model

next. In Mary's practice, this error in communicating has happened so much that she and a colleague designed an effective execution program called High Performance Leadership™, which teaches supervisors and managers how to communicate performance expectations, coach, and follow up with others in the spirit of building a high-performing organization. Participants learn how to translate expectations into behaviors and results and how to have conversations with those they lead when performance is good and when it is less than acceptable. Figure 2 illustrates the High Performance Leadership model.

One of the things we've found in building a high-performing company is that you need to start with what's important to all employees in terms of what they enjoy doing, what motivates them, and what their dreams are. If you do this, you can then show how what you expect sometimes ties into what is purposeful work for them. A focus on learning what's important to those who work for you helps you engage others at a deep level and build significance for them. An example of how well this simple process works is described by one of the CEOs we talked with.

Michael was hired to run a company after his predecessor failed. Morale was terrible and performance was at an all-time low. Immediately, he made time to talk with each employee to get to know them and to hear about their goals and aspirations. He asked for their ideas on how the organization could be more effective, and when it made sense, he implemented the suggestions. With an open approach and a genuine interest in others, this new CEO and the organization went on to achieve record levels of performance and team spirit.

In his book *It's Your Ship,* Captain Michael Abrashoff talks about how his ship, the USS *Benfold,* went from the worst performer in the Pacific fleet to the best in nine months. One of the secrets of Abrashoff's success, and something that created significance for his crew, was his taking the time to get to know each crew member. Abrashoff learned about each person's dreams and goals; when appropriate he considered these in making work assignments and in creating opportunities for development and growth. The results were amazing—close to flawless execution (Abrashoff, 2002).

One of the insights Darrel shared with Joe was to *hold people accountable for their personal and team objectives and give them the space to innovate.* By involving others in the development of relevant objectives and action plans, you set the stage for accountability. You draw a box with boundaries set by the expectations you agree to, and you can then leave the individual or team to work innovatively toward meeting each objective. Mary will often ask a group to think about a time when the work they did was so engaging that time flew, they were excited about getting to work, and they felt energized by what they were doing. Once people hold a mental picture of that experience, she asks them, "Where was your supervisor during that time?" The answer is consistently, "Nowhere to be found."

Setting up specific expectations and coming to agreement allows others to then have the autonomy to innovate. In addition, the organization's values serve as guidelines for how to go about achieving your objectives and goals so the "what," or results, and "how," or behaviors, of high performance are clear.

- *The leaders develop capabilities and rewards and recognize high performance formally and informally.*

The most successful organizations constantly assess their capabilities against what needs to get done, starting with their vision. In high-performing organizations, the leadership is able to compare the current reality with their plan: "Where is the company now in relation to our vision and overall strategy?" They get input from stakeholders at all levels of the company so they can realistically assess the organization's current state. Key stakeholders are enlisted to analyze the gap between where the organization is now and where it wants to be or its preferred future. Assess your capabilities as part of this analysis. Capabilities involve having the right people, processes, and relational systems in place to support your plan. Ask questions such as "Do we have the right number and mix of people to support our plan?" "Does our current structure align with and support effective execution?" and "How do our work processes align with what needs to get done?" Answering these and related questions honestly can make a big difference in how well you perform now and in the future.

To build a high-performing organization, examine what the organization is rewarding and recognizing, and make sure that what gets rewarded supports your plan. Mary has worked with more than one organization that says it wants to build teamwork, yet most of the formal and informal reward and recognition systems reinforce individual behavior and results. Or, an organization may institute a profit-sharing plan in the spirit of rewarding and recognizing great performance; yet the plan backfires because people can't see the relationship between their efforts (on an individual or team basis) and the company's bottom line. Sometimes when the whole organization is recognized through an annual bonus, an opportunity to accelerate the plan is missed because people can't see their impact on reaching the plan.

One of the CEOs Mary has worked with, Gary Treat, owns a commercial air-conditioning franchise. He instituted an open-book management process in which employees learn about the financials, what drives them, and how what they do as a team can have an impact. He rewards employees financially and emotionally through recognition events. What separates this approach from a blanket profit-sharing plan is specificity showing employees just what they as a team need to accomplish to share in the rewards. Because the company financials are available to everyone who works there, employees become owners in a sense. They also learn who is contributing and who is struggling, or worse, not participating; this information allows everyone to monitor one another, coach, or pressure their peers to do better. Treat has found a process that creates a culture of accountability, and his business has grown exponentially over the past five years. Treat calls his approach the "Great Game" (Stack 1994). "The key element to the success of our 'Great Game' is the training workshop that allows everyone to learn what is important to win in our business," Treat explains. "People want to be successful. The 'Great Game' is a tool that shows them how, and provides a financial reward when we win."

A Broader View

We've talked about how to engage others to execute with excellence. Beyond achieving your plan and the results you want, how do you widen your view and create significance for yourself and for those you lead? Many CEOs must hit rock bottom or experience a life-threatening event, such as facing cancer, for them to stop and think about what a successful and meaningful life means to them. Like Joe, the changing environment forces contemplation, perhaps for the first time. Rather than take the long and hard road, consider the following.

- When you have a new idea you want to execute, go back to your mission, vision, values, and core focus to make sure the new idea fits.

- Remember that real and enduring success is about the sum total of the actions, activities, and events in your life, so consider the long-term implications of what you plan to do next.

- Three categories help sort through what needs to be part of a meaningful life.
  - *Achievement:* whatever you want to excel at or accomplish in your life
  - *Happiness:* whatever brings you joy
  - *Legacy:* going from success to significance—the impact of the gift you want to leave behind (see Chapter 8)

Jim Ferman Jr., the CEO of Ferman Motor Car Company, has been able to execute well in the business started more than a hundred years ago by his grandfather, W. F. Ferman. Here is what he says:

My major accomplishment was growing a business that was based on an old model and brought this family business into a new generation. I see my legacy as being a bridge between several generations. . . . I define success in terms of balance. My personal mission statement is very similar to the organization's—it involves the successful balancing of time, talent, and treasure—this means career, family, community, and self, as well as spiritual dimensions.

The Right Execution at Home

Living what you preach is doubly critical at home, where accountability can be even more difficult than it is at your company. "I sent all the right messages at the office and all the wrong ones at home," says one CEO.

My kids couldn't understand why they couldn't do all the cool things their wealthy friends were doing when I had just bought a new car and new boat and other toys. All the child experts say that "do as I say, not as I do" never works, so it was really dumb of me to expect a different result. When I started to sit down and have talks with them about "planting and sowing," they connected the dots of working hard to get what you want. I also used a youth coach who sent the same messages I had tried to send, but was perceived as more credible than Mom or Dad.

Good execution with raising children can pay off handsomely in the future. Gene and Lena Corrigan shared the significance goal of raising their seven children to be honest, hardworking, and contributors to society in a way consistent with each child's skills and life interests. Gene and Lena spent time every week talking and figuring out how they would coach each child, all of whom had different personalities and different challenges along the way. "Gene was gone a lot during the early years of his career, and the children constantly tested my resolve and his," says Lena.

> When one of our children crossed the line, if they tried to go around my punishment by appealing to Dad, Gene would always back me up, even if he felt guilty about having been away and was inclined to lessen the punishment. This was one of the key reasons we executed our Significance Plan successfully, along with loving our kids unconditionally despite their testing our patience all the time. Our children have fulfilled our dreams for significance many times over and are passing those good child-rearing execution skills down to our grandchildren, which is a wonderful blessing for them and for us.

Surveys often cite money as one of the top causes of divorce, which is itself one of the top five threats to financial independence, because most people are saving barely enough to support two people, and not nearly enough for the two living separately. When two spouses are of different minds on budgeting, spending on their toys versus the kids' needs, and so on, *having an independent planner to help sort out execution priorities* can be valuable. Choose someone who listens to both parties and looks for balanced solutions. Too often a Type A CEO will dominate personal planning meetings with planners, investment advisors, attorneys, CPAs, and other advisors. A less-knowledgeable spouse or life partner may disagree with decisions being made, sit quietly and not provide much input, and then sabotage the execution plan later on. Letting an experienced financial planner explore internal and external finance issues equally and then educate the family member with less knowledge or experience will often help successfully carry out personal execution goals.

Budgeting is another key area in which couples can disagree on execution, even if they have agreed in their Significance Plan that having a sound retirement, providing extra funds for favorite charities, and helping children start a business or buy a home are important to the success of their joint plan. Private company CEOs often reinvest profits to grow the Golden Goose to the exclusion of creature comforts. When they become more successful, they often retain the frugal approach that got them to success, while their life partner may feel it is time to "reap what has been sowed." The best way to resolve this kind of issue is to create the kind of highly visual plan described in Right Planning and to make sure both partners have contributed to its creation and fully understand the dynamics of how decisions on various kinds of spending affect longer-term significance goals. Just as you want your employees to be doing the right thing to move the organization toward its goals when you're not around to watch them, you also want the entire family (including you) making decisions within the context of a unified plan.

At times, bringing in a professional to help guide the process is even more critical for successfully executing a lifetime Significance Plan. What if you and your life partner disagree about a key area of your combined Significance Plan to the point that it may jeopardize your relationship?

A good example of this is a CEO, Jack, and his wife, Dorothy, whom Dennis has worked with for more than fifteen years. Jack wanted to give a six-figure gift to his college, partly wanting to give back and partly wanting to keep up with his friends who were donating large sums. (Secretly, he also wanted to get great basketball and football tickets.) Dorothy thought it was an ego trip for Jack and didn't see the significance in the gift at all. She wanted to reserve the money to help several struggling charities she worked with that she felt were both more deserving and less able to fend for themselves.

Dennis talked to the college and determined what they needed to get Jack the benefits he desired. He also interviewed the executive directors of Dorothy's favorite charities and found out what they needed to help accomplish their goals. Jack and Dorothy ended up splitting the charitable gift into a lifetime and an estate (at death) portion for both Jack's college and Dorothy's nonprofit groups. Some couples can figure out these kinds of conflicts on their own, whereas others will need the help of a planner/facilitator to keep the debate over what is significant more focused and less emotional.

Just as with organizations, celebrate the achievement of personal milestones in your Significance Plan. Part of the fun in life is to enjoy the abundance that comes to you. The most fulfilled of our CEOs were people who, like Jack and Dorothy, also remembered others in giving back.

•

Get input from the entire company, as well as from key stakeholders outside the company, on where your organization is in relation to the plan and how you need to get there.

•

Develop observable, measurable, and verifiable objectives for teams and individuals that support your plan and that set a standard for excellence.

•

Determine how **you want to acknowledge and reward people** for meeting and exceeding their objectives.

•

Everyone in your company needs to know that executing on commitments and supporting their success are your priorities; you demonstrate this through your actions. **Ask performance-related questions, seek ideas, and place an emphasis on achieving agreed-on results.**

•

Make accountability and excellent performance priorities, and set up a reward and recognition system that supports reaching performance expectations.

•

Personal execution by you and your family should be guided by a shared vision of the future. Where the vision isn't in sync, at least make sure your family resolves conflicts well so one roadblock doesn't get the entire families' Significance Plan off track.

•

Do as I say, not as I do will lead to failure and potential disaster in both your business and personal lives. Your family and your employees closely watch how your words and deeds match up every single day. Right Execution depends on keeping values, policies, and execution aligned.

CHAPTER

8

THE RIGHT LEGACY

Webster's dictionary defines "robots" as "mechanical devices operating automatically, in a seemingly human way." It's no accident that Joe was attracted to robotics. He discovered, like so many of the CEOs we've interviewed and worked with, that being driven to achieve in your career can suck the humanity out of you. When you're so focused on only one thing, there's a dangerous tendency to live life automatically, without reflection.

Often, the outside world reinforces the idea that achievement should be the only value in life, since many CEOs appear to be successful and have the admiration of others for it. But making work goals the only, or even the main, priority can damage friendships, marriages, and relationships with children. John, self-made head of a $500 million private company, knows this fact all too well. He laments, "I fooled myself into thinking that I was working hard for my kids so they would want for nothing. I didn't spend the kind of time with them that I should have. Now they're grown, and they rarely make an effort to see me. I'm top on their list, though, if they need money."

Make no mistake: the idea of leaving a legacy in life didn't usually occur to our CEOs until one of three things happened:

- They had a life crisis, such as the loss of a spouse or partner through divorce or death, or they experienced life-threatening health challenges themselves or with those they love.

- They went through a midlife crisis and wondered, "Is this all there is?"

- They grew spiritually, realizing that those things that were once so important, such as wealth and power, were secondary to feeling a connection to God and humanity.

Another of our CEOs, Dave, worked for a large accounting staffing company and then started his own business, which grew into a major player in the IT and accounting staffing business. "Initially, work consumed me," he said. "I felt I had to control everything to be effective. After a failed marriage and much soul-searching, I nurtured my faith. I made my spiritual beliefs a priority, and now I'm able to let go more in business and delegate." Today, Dave accepts the influence of a Higher

Power in his life. Serving God and others is now what he considers his legacy. His mantra is "to those whom much is given, much is expected."

Like Dave, many high achievers realize that success alone is hollow without creating significance in their life and in the lives of others. Our interviews and work with CEOs confirms that, eventually, some of them made a shift from success thinking to significance thinking. Significance thinking involves asking oneself, "What is the impact of the gift I want to leave behind?" This is what we are calling legacy.

Legacy can be physical in nature, such as an architecturally pleasing building; relational, such as raising children; or intellectual, such as a book or patent. For example, most parents want to raise their children to be loving and productive contributors to the planet. Some people's legacy is the effect they've had on society or some slice of it, such as one of our CEOs who sees his business as affecting others through the company's modeling of socially responsible business practices, even if they cost more.

Legacy can also be spiritual. A leader can model and teach values such as integrity that become a way of life for future generations. Think of the legacy people like Mother Teresa, Martin Luther King Jr., and Mahatma Gandhi left us. They probably never sat down with pen and paper to map out their legacy, yet their visionary leadership and ability to model their values created legacy far beyond what they probably ever imagined. These heroes have left us the gift of inspiration and the hope that no matter what the situation, if you are clear on what's really important, anything is possible.

Legacy can also be sinister and dark. Few would argue that Adolf Hitler, Idi Amin, and Saddam Hussein didn't leave a legacy of hatred and separation. On the corporate level, thousands lost their life savings and were betrayed by the greed and deception of the CEO and other leaders of companies such as Enron, Tyco, and World-Com. With the exposure of so many corporate scandals, we have become cynical about CEOs. Is it still possible for CEOs to be seen as capable of leaving a positive legacy for others?

The media myth claims that the charisma and personal brand of celebrity CEOs can carry them and their organizations to new heights. In fact, the opposite is true. Jim Collins and others have dispelled this myth of the "rock star CEO." As these experts assert, truly successful CEOs of some of the best companies keep a low profile and step out of the limelight to give credit to the entire team when the organization is successful. Unlike many celebrity CEOs who deflect personal responsibility when things go wrong, the more effective CEOs take personal responsibility.

The best company leaders understand the power of purposeful work and find a way to connect the personal passions and values of others with a compelling purpose and vision for the organization and beyond. Instead of just stating what their values are, higher-level leaders act on their values. They consistently communicate and model their values in their daily life—at work, at home, in the community, and anywhere else they happen to be. For example, if a leader claims integrity as a core value, then you should be able to see behaviors that display integrity as part of the way he or she leads and conducts business, including telling the truth, listening to others with respect, and doing the right thing, even if it costs more. Over time, modeling or living your values becomes the CEO's legacy. You become the sum total of the behaviors you model and use to interact with people in your environment. Stated simply, Values + Action = Legacy.

John West started a technology staffing company, System One, in 1987. When he sold his company in 2000 and looked back on his major accomplishments, what stood out to John was the number of people who worked for him who eventually started their own companies. "I believe the reason for others becoming entrepreneurs was that I taught them how to run their part of the business as if it were their own, and I was available to support and mentor them." At the core of his philosophy were the System One values he and other leaders committed to modeling. They developed these values into the acronym

HIRED (*H*onor, *I*ntegrity, *R*espect, *E*nthusiasm, and *D*edication). Former employees who went on to start their own businesses made these values part of the way their organizations did business.

When asked what they saw as their legacy, more than 60 percent of our CEOs responded, *developing others as leaders*. Many commented that knowing that those they mentored went on to do great things was very fulfilling. Several said that the impact of developing leaders was exponential and that being part of that development was exhilarating. "It makes me so proud to see the impact of those I've mentored. They have gone on to be so much better than I see myself as being," commented one of our CEOs.

Another former CEO we interviewed also saw her legacy as developing others: "I just loved working with so many talented people on what we thought was right," commented Jan Alpert, who was president of LandAmerica Financial Group, Inc., from 1993 through 2003. Jan began her career at a time when it was even more difficult for a woman to rise to an executive leadership role than it is today. Her company was at $10 million in revenues when she started, and it grew to $3 billion in revenues through acquisition and by focusing on leadership development. Jan would often coach other women on how to move up the corporate ladder. "Apply for new roles, always develop your successor, and be persistent," she'd advise. "I see my biggest contribution as coaching others to be their personal best," Jan says. By all accounts, Jan was a great model for developing top talent. Companies like GE have left a legacy with their outstanding management development programs. GE alums continue to be sought after to head companies because of their rich leadership experiences and the emphasis they place on accountability and mentoring others.

In an interview with Mary, system change expert Peter Senge commented that the most meaningful commitment leaders and organizations can make is to support the sustainability of our planet. Peter cites Unilever as an example of a company concerned with sustaining agriculture, fishing, and a healthy water supply. As companies assess possible future world scenarios, they are realizing that stewardship of the planet's resources is essential to our long-term survival.

John Brown of BP has made counteracting global warming a priority. BP is now the second largest investor in solar energy. The Body Shop is another example of positive corporate legacy. Founder Anita Roddick has helped people around the world live productive lives because her company places a priority on purchasing raw materials and handcrafted items from indigenous peoples. The Body Shop's economic model allows people in remote parts of the world to live and prosper while preserving many rich traditions that would almost certainly die out otherwise.

Developing a Legacy

Many of us have been reassessing what's important in life and how we can as individuals live a life that matters. "How can we dedicate energy to those things that are more personally fulfilling?" becomes a lingering question as we struggle to balance a search for meaning with pressing time commitments to work and family life and the frantic pace at which we live.

According to psychologist Erik Erikson, we go through developmental stages at certain points in our lives. If we don't accomplish the development task of each stage, our ability to adjust to life's challenges can go awry. For example, developmentally, people age forty to sixty-five can experience a life crisis if they don't feel they have created some kind of a legacy by having children, making an impact on the next generation in some way, or creating something for posterity. If people don't achieve this stage of generativity, Erikson states, they stagnate in their life. It's no wonder significance is on the minds of Baby Boomers, and will be on the minds of Generations X and Y as they age.

From his work on what separates great companies from the rest, Jim Collins has picked ten top CEOs. All of his selections share the characteristic of going beyond personal self-interest to build something greater for the company, its customers, and society. Collins points out that the "level 5 leader" is both personally humble and fiercely focused on success and accountability for the company. Collins describes this leader as an "individual who blends extreme personal humility with intense professional will."

The five levels of leadership were based on observations that Collins and his team documented in *Good to Great*. There, the level 1 leader is defined as a highly capable individual who contributes to the company through talent and skills; level 2 is a contributing member of a team who enhances the team in reaching its objectives; level 3 is a competent manager who organizes people and resources in reaching agreed-on objectives; and level 4 is an effective leader who is able to gain commitment toward the attainment of a compelling vision and objectives.

Research shows that exceptional leadership enables companies to go from good to stellar. Is there also a relationship between legacy and level 5 leadership? In our research of CEOs, we found that about 15 percent of those we surveyed could be categorized as true level 5 leaders and many were solid level 4 leaders. The level 5 CEOs stated that what really mattered wasn't what "I did" but what "we did together" that had a positive impact on others and the world.

Guy King, the CEO of M. E. Wilson, a property and casualty family insurance business started by his father, is an example of the "we did it together" attitude that is characteristic of the level 5 leader. He sees his and the organization's legacy as the fulfillment of the company's mission, which is "to reward our loyal team members that deliver outstanding value to our clients and partners in a 'best practices' environment." As King says, "Helping others become successful and creating significance for them is my overriding goal. In turn, employees are willing to go the extra mile for the company." This commitment has been recognized by others: M. E. Wilson has won numerous awards for displaying excellence, being a great place to work, and modeling humanitarian practices.

Four Levels of Legacy

It might be helpful to think about legacy in levels as well, although the levels are not sequential inherently. We could, however, categorize what the CEOs we interviewed saw as their legacies into four areas.

- *Physical legacy,* such as building financial independence for themselves and their families, erecting a building such as the Trump Tower, endowing a chair at a university, or having children
- *Intellectual legacy,* such as writing a book or developing patents
- *Emotional or social legacy,* such as improving the quality of life for employees through friendly work practices, instituting state-of-the-art environmental processes, and raising responsible family members

- *Spiritual legacy,* such as living your values every day, not looking for any reward—just, in some way, leaving the world a better place.

These levels are not mutually exclusive. Some of our CEOs mentioned legacies that fell into more than one category. One of the CEOs we interviewed, Dr. Kirin Patel, came to this country to start a medical practice with his wife, also a doctor. He grew up in an Indian family and lived in Africa as a child. He was raised in a home in which his father placed an emphasis on helping others, particularly family and the poor. "My father was an inspiration. He taught me that the more you gain in life, so grows your responsibility for others." Patel has started and built many medically related businesses. He gives generously to his relatives, the community, and beyond. His foundation funds school programs, the arts, development of global understanding, and more. In addition to the social legacy he is leaving, Patel believes that on a spiritual level, it's important "to touch others in a positive way so that you are contributing to making the world a better place for others." He strongly believes that teaching others how to make a difference in their own life is one of the greatest gifts you can give.

Think one person can't change the world? The breadth of some legacies is so vast, they're difficult to describe. Wade Hatcher, the former CEO of a successful medical practice and an accomplished surgeon, did much to change the world, as you will see from just a sampling of stories those whose lives he touched. So great were his life and legacy that they continue to influence and inspire others long after his passing from this world.

Many sought Wade's advice on all manner of subjects, from relationships with friends to dealing with their children to looking at business opportunities to how to fix a tractor. He kept in touch with people he had operated on and with operating room nurses he had worked with thirty years ago. He would have lunch with an out-of-work handyman, helping him regroup, and then have dinner with the mayor that evening.

Wade literally died with his boots on at age seventy-four after retiring to Colorado with his wife and soul mate, Jan. After his death, 300 friends and family members held a "Celebration of Life" for Wade. People shared how he had touched and changed their lives: by being a great listener, by keeping his word, by communicating through storytelling to open up new ways of looking at things.

A former patient said of Wade,

> I came in for some surgery, but Wade could tell I had more on my mind and gently asked what was really the matter. My son was dealing with drugs and a failed job and wouldn't take advice from his parents or anyone. My wife had gone into depression over the situation, so our marriage was strained. Wade listened longer than most

friends would have and certainly took more time than any doctor. He helped me understand how to comfort my wife. He called my son into his office to talk about my medical condition. After explaining the risks of my surgery, he got my son talking about himself. Thirty minutes later, my son had an appointment with a therapist, a drug counselor, and a friend of Wade's who was willing to give him a job and a break. My son is now a manager of this fellow's company and has a wife and two children. He has been clean and sober for over fifteen years. My wife and I have had a wonderful marriage and enjoy our grand-babies. I came in to see Wade and have my arteries repaired and left having my entire life repaired.

"Wade would always listen intently to what you had to say," said another friend.

You knew you had his undivided attention. Half the time, I figured a problem out myself just by talking to him! There's something about talking with a wise man that makes you wiser in the bargain. The other half of the time he would ask questions and help you think through the problem. And the huge network of friends he had meant he could get somebody else into the discussion who might have the answer, even if he didn't. He was always learning, always trying to make himself better. Wade really tried to help turn people's lives around; he didn't always succeed, but most of the time he made a real difference.

"Wade taught me how to deal with people, not directly, but just by being around him and watching him interact with people," said Mary, one of his nurses.

He taught me you can communicate with just about anyone if you listen long and hard enough to figure out what makes them tick. The best part was, I started attracting a much better type of man in my dating by using some of Wade's communication techniques. I met the man of my dreams, married, and had children. Boy, were listening and understanding skills ever needed then! So many near-crisis situations ended up positive when I know they could have been disasters. Without Wade's mentoring, even though he never really knew he was doing it, my life could have turned out so much worse. Instead, it just keeps getting better and better!

We will never really know how many marriages have been kept on the Right Road, how many children have been led to the Right Road, and how many people have been able to cope better or seize opportunities because one person made an effort every single day. That was one of Wade's visions for his legacy: powerful, lasting change that makes a difference in the world.

Every time you interact with an employee, a friend, your life partner, or a family member, you touch a life that touches dozens of others every day. Every time you can inject optimism, faith in the future, and wisdom, you help make a difference. If you inspire those around you with your positive words and deeds, you will create positive ripples that will grow into large waves of loyalty, trust, and love over time.

Successful CEOs who report feeling fulfilled in their life are multifaceted. They look at their life, achievements, and contributions through a lens of diverse and connected goals or areas of importance. They have learned how to focus on one area of their life, such as being more competitive in the marketplace, and then shift priorities to focus on another, such as enjoying times with family and friends.

•

Position your company for long-term success *and* **significance.** Make sure you have the best and brightest people doing *purposeful work;* this will free up time and focus for you to pursue a higher level of significance in your business, with your family, and with other personal pursuits.

•

Help mentor others and develop talent within the organization. This is a good idea for all areas of your life since it strengthens your networks and the people around you who can help you make your dreams come true.

•

Positively affect community organizations and beyond through your company's generosity in dollars, time, and access to resources. Being a "good citizen" is important to enhance the quality of life where you, your family, and your employees live.

•

Be a Great Leader—level 3 or 4 will probably get you to your destination, but **striving for level 5 makes it more likely you and your company will achieve both success and significance.** Level 5 leaders are both personally humble and fiercely focused on goals and accountability.

•

Make your organization an employer of choice. If you follow the Right Focus, Right People, Right Execution approach to your business, it will be an attractive place to work, which will further enhance your success and possibilities of achieving your Significance Goals.

•

Write a speech now for your last day at work and describe your organization's greatest contribution. Then write your eulogy and notice how much time you spend talking about the company versus your family, friends, and community.

•

Ask: How will our company contribute to the greater good of society? The world? How can you create products and services that improve the lives of your company's customers and accomplish your financial goals for the company?

•

Consider how many lives you could affect if you model significance along with success. **Like ripples in a pond, your helping to positively influence others multiplies.**

EPILOGUE

Joe felt as if he were floating. He opened his eyes to darkness, sitting up and looking down to see that there really was nothing beneath him. He panicked for a second, thinking, "*Now I'm dead? In limbo or something? After all that? Now, that would be ironic.*"

He stood upright, though there was no discernable floor beneath him, and he felt just as light and balanced as when he was lying down. He realized he was smiling in the darkness, his joy welling up from somewhere deep within. "Wow," he whispered. "So this is what inner peace feels like. Huh . . ."

Far away, it seemed, a door opened up and a growing triangle of light flooded in. He heard heavy footsteps while his eyes adjusted, and then there was his partner, George, right in front of him.

"George," he said, evenly, trying to conceal his even greater happiness at now seeing his old friend.

"Joe," George replied, rather sternly.

"You always were a scoundrel," Joe said, smiling and shaking his head. "And you always knew me too well. I don't know how I can thank you for this experience, for making this happen. I don't know if you even know what you've given me."

"Given you and a lot of other people, too, huh?"

"Oh, yes! I feel like I finally understand everything that I missed before, all the wrong turns I made. Tell me I'm going to get a chance to make it right. There's so much I feel like I need to do . . . that I *want* to do . . ." His voice trailed off, half-expectant, half-afraid of George's severe look.

Suddenly, George smiled, that big goofy smile Joe hadn't seen for many years, the look he used to get in the early, heady days when they were planning to take Chiron International to the top. "Aw" George laughed. "You always were a smart one, Joe. You listened real good this time for once and you *got* it, I can tell. You definitely ran off the road, in more ways than one. But now you can get back on, and stay on, even find the scenic route, if you take what you learned to heart. Now's the time to get moving on all of this stuff."

"You're right, George. I want to get started right away. How do I start?"

"Now you can really go places, do all that stuff we wanted to do in the beginning. Give Sam and Tony a call, why don't you? Get out there and make it right: with them, with the company, with that pretty wife of yours, and with your great kid. Build a future, now that you got a second shot at one."

"I will, partner, I will, but I'm kind of here and all that's there, and . . . "

And then, suddenly, he wasn't *there*, wherever there was, anymore. He was lying in a hospital bed, a pale yellow curtain pulled around it. "Okay," he whispered. "Bye, George. Thank you so much."

"Joe?" He was startled to hear Sharon's voice. "Joe? Are you really awake? How do you feel? Oh, God, the doctors were saying they had no idea when you'd wake up, if you'd wake up. How do you feel? Can you talk? Did you just say something about George?"

Joe looked at his wife. He felt such love for her, just as he had in their first years together. He realized she was clutching his hand, and he squeezed hers. He wondered for a moment if this were real, if she was really there or just another vision. Either way, he had a lot to say, if only he could figure out how to say it.

"I'm sorry," he heard himself say. That was a good start. "For everything."

"Let's not get into that now, Joe. I need to go tell the doctor you're awake," Sharon said, standing and starting to move away from the bed.

"No, let me just say something first. I feel like I'm just bursting, Sharon. I have to say this."

"Okay," she said, somewhat nervously, and sat again next to the bed.

"It's just this: I love you and Collin so much. So much more than I let you know, so much more than anything else in the whole world. I have a lot to make up for, and I know you won't believe this, but I hope you'll try: I am going to be a partner to you again. I am going to listen to you, really listen. I know this probably sounds crazy, and I can't really explain it right now. But I see everything differently now. I hope you can find some way to give me a chance. I will do *anything* in the world to try to make things right with us. I need you and Collin, and I know I haven't given you both anything even close to what *you* need, but that will change. You just have to find a way to give me a chance."

Sharon stared at him. "Wow. I don't know what to say."

Joe laughed. "I didn't either, believe it or not! That's just what came out, and it turns out that's *just* what I wanted to say. Can you just tell me what you feel?"

"I can hardly believe it, but I feel like saying 'Okay.' I can tell that you're sincere. I feel like you're the old Joe, the one I fell in love with. And I want so much for our family to work again. I'm scared, but I'm willing to take the chance." Sharon leaned over the bed and kissed him fervently.

"Oh, you must be so thirsty. Let me go get water and tell the doctor you're awake." She grinned slyly and asked, "Is it wrong for me to be wishing you'd had a horrible car crash a few years earlier? Oh, that is so bad!"

"No," Joe laughed. "I know what you mean. I kind of feel the same way, honey."

Sharon slipped through the curtains, and Joe fumbled on the nightstand for a phone. He thought for a minute and punched in the familiar number.

Tony answered the phone on the first ring. "Hello?"

"Tony, it's Joe."

Tony responded with silence.

"Look, Tony, I know this is going to sound crazy, what I have to say, but do you think you can bear with me for a minute?"

After a long pause, Tony finally answered, "I suppose."

"You have every right to be angry and hurt, but please try to hear what I have to say. I've had a pretty amazing day."

"Good for you."

"Well, not like you think, but it *has* been good for me, and it will be good for you, too. I need to say that I get it now, Tony, everything you and Sam told me all along. I know I've done a lot of damage to our relationship, and I want to do what I can to repair that damage. I fully understand why you and Sam felt cheated, that you did so much for the company—you gave 100 percent—and yet you didn't have anything to show for it. Then I went and fired you! I can't change the past, the way I treated you both, but I can show you that *I* have changed. I'm calling to ask both of you to come back. I want you to be my partners. And I want us to create the vision we all once shared of Chiron International as *the* innovator in the robotics industry. We can help others in the process too, Tony, I know it. We're going to change lives with our technology, just like we planned. We'll never settle for less than the best, ever again. The whole organization is going to determine our mission, our vision, our values, and decide what we can be best at . . . I know this is a lot to absorb right now . . ."

"No kidding."

"But will you at least think about it? Will you talk to Sam and come see me whenever you're ready?"

"I don't understand. What's this all about? What brought about this change?"

"You wouldn't believe me if I told you, Tony. I don't quite believe it myself, but it doesn't matter. What matters is that I *have* changed and, together, we're going to make a difference—if you'll join me."

"Well, I can't say I'm not intrigued. Sam and I have some free time these days. How about we meet in the morning?"

"That's great, Tony. Thank you. Only don't come to my office. I think my office is going to be in Parkview Hospital for a few days."

"What?"

Joe looked up to see Sharon and a doctor pulling back the yellow curtain around the bed. "Look, I have to go, Tony. But bring Sam tomorrow morning to Parkview. And, buddy, please drive carefully, OK?"

REFERENCES

Abrashoff, Captain D. Michael. *It's Your Ship.* New York: Warner Books, 2002.

Bossidy, Larry, and Ram Charan. *Execution.* New York: Crown Business (Random House, Inc.), 2002.

Byham, William C. *The Selection Solution.* Bridgeville, Pa.: Development Dimensions International, 1996.

Collins, James C. *Good to Great.* New York: HarperCollins, 2001.

Collins, James C., and Jerry I. Porras. *Built to Last.* New York: HarperCollins, 1997.

Covey, Stephen R. *The 8th Habit.* New York: Free Press, 2004.

Fritz, Robert. *The Path of Least Resistance.* New York: Ballantine Books, 1989.

Key, Mary H.. and Laura Capp. *High-Performance Leadership.* Self-published training program, 2002

Loehr, James E. *Toughness Training for Life.* New York: Penguin Group, 1993.

Loehr, Jim, and Tony Schwartz. *The Power of Full Engagement.* New York: Free Press, 2003.

Manz, Charles C., Karen P. Manz, Robert D. Marx, and Christopher P. Neck. *The Wisdom of Solomon.* San Francisco: Berrett-Koehler, 2001.

McCann, Joseph. "Organizational Effectiveness: Changing Concepts for Changing Environments," *Human Resource Planning* 27(1), April 2004, pp. 42-50.

Nanus, Burt. *Visionary Leadership.* New York: Jossey-Bass, 1995.

Nash, Laura, and Howard Stevenson. *Just Enough.* Hoboken, N.J.: John Wiley & Sons, 2004.

Senge, Peter. *The Fifth Discipline.* New York: Doubleday, 1990.

Stack, Jack. *The Great Game of Business.* New York: Random House, 1994.

Weisbord, Marvin, and Sandra Janoff. *Future Search: An Action Guide to Finding Common Ground in Organizations and Communities.* San Francisco: Berrett-Koehler, 1995.

INDEX

Abrashoff, Michael, 158
accountability: as priority, 169; for
    personal and team objectives,
    159; in values system, 61–62
achievement, 89–90, 94, 162, 171
action plans, 159
Alpert, Jan, 176
assertiveness, 104

behaviors: modeling of, 151–153;
    past, 102, 120
Bodaken, Bruce, 57–58
Bodford, Al, 63–64, 116
Bontempo, Leo, 156
Brown, John, 177
Bruce, David, 114
budgeting, 165

candidates: evaluations of,
    100–106; interview of, 102–104;
    past behaviors of, 102, 120

capabilities, 160
celebrity CEOs, 174
change: abrupt, 139–140; descrip-
    tion of, 123; disruptive, 125,
    135; mental toughness for,
    125–130, 144; rate of, 136;
    real-time, 156; resiliency to,
    123
charisma, 174
children, 141–143
Circumstance, Action, Result (CAR)
    approach, 102
coaching, developmental, 106–108,
    120
collaboration, 60
collective intelligence, 135
Collie, Joe, 72–73
Collins, Jim, 64–65, 178
commitment, 68, 168
communicating of vision, 153
community organizations, 186

competencies, 101-102
conflict, 61
coping, 139
core focus, 64-66
core values, 63-64, 175
Corrigan, Gene, 56-57, 112
Covey, Stephen, 150
creativity, 139
crisis: description of, 127-128;
   legacy and, 172
crisis planning, 139-141

Dale, Jerry, 76-77
decision making, 156
Dermody, Win, 117-118, 129-130
developmental coaching, 106-108,
   120
diet, 133
disruptive change, 125, 135
diversity, 60
Dougherty, Michael, 52, 61, 71,
   133, 153
Dubois, Blanche, 155
Duke, Peter, 128-129, 141
Dunkel, Dave, 154

economics, 87
emotional intelligence, 104-106
emotional legacy, 180
empathy, 105
employee retention, 52
empowerment, 156
Erikson, Erik, 178
excellence, 60
execution: failure of, 150-151;
   at home, 163-167; principles
   of, 150-161. See also Right
   Execution
executive coach, 110
exercise, 133

expectations, modeling of, 152
experience-based learning, 144
external planning, 87-88

feedback, 110, 149, 154
Ferman, Jim Jr., 162-163
Feuerstein, Aaron, 124
fight-or-flight response, 126
financial planning, 86-92
Fritz, Robert, 131

goals: attainment of, 132, 159;
   defining of, 154; setting of, 89
Great Game, 161
group interview, 102

Haines, Bill, 131
happiness, 89, 94
Hatcher, Wade, 181-184
Hedgehog Concept, 64-65
Heineman, Peter, 127, 132-133,
   149
high performance, 160
High Performance Leadership
   model, 157
hiring: candidate evaluation,
   100-106; emotional intelligence
   and, 104-106; individuals
   involved in, 102-103; poor fit
   in, 99-100; selection process,
   99-100; urgency in, 99
home: interdependencies at,
   137-138; Right Execution at,
   163-167
home team, 111-113
humor, 133-134

implementation plan, 155
impulse control, 105
innovation, 60

integrity, 60, 175
intellectual legacy, 180
interdependencies: at home,
    137–138; in organization, 135
interviews, 102–104

Jacobs, Sheldon, 74
judgment, 101–102

Kelleher, Herb, 104
key stakeholders, 155, 160
King, Guy, 179–180

Lankins, John, 75
laughter, 134
Lea, Rhea, 106
leader: capabilities developed by,
    160; developing of, as legacy,
    175–176; execution by,
    154–159; high performance
    recognized by, 160; levels of,
    178–179; modeling of behavior
    by, 151–153
leadership levels, 179, 187
learning: experience-based, 144;
    focus on, 158; scenario, 79–86,
    141
learning organization, 134–135
legacy: description of, 89–90, 94,
    162; development of, 178–180;
    emotional, 180; examples of,
    184–185; intellectual, 180;
    leader development as, 176;
    levels of, 180–185; modeling of
    behaviors by, 175; physical,
    173, 180; reasons for leaving,
    172; sinister, 174; social, 180;
    spiritual, 173–174, 181
life balance, 89
life crisis, 172, 178

life partner, 78
Loehr, James, 125–126

Mason, Steve, 107
meaning in life, 162
megatrends, 136
mental toughness, 125–130, 144
mentor, 77–78, 186
midlife crisis, 172
mission: description of, 50–53;
    self-assessments, 67–68; vision
    vs., 53
mission statement: description of,
    50; vision statement vs., 58–59
modeling: of behaviors, 151–153;
    of expectations, 152

network team, 109–111
networking: for next generation,
    118–119; for personal success,
    116–118; for Right People,
    113–116; tips for, 121
next generation, 118–119
nutrition, 133–134

objectives, 154–155, 159, 168
online learning, 85
opportunities, 136, 142
organization: collective intelli-
    gence of, 135; high-performing,
    160; interdependencies in, 135;
    learning, 134–135; purpose of,
    175; recognition of, 161

past baggage, 74–75, 93
past behaviors, 102, 120
Patel, Kirin, 181
patterns, 85
peer advisory board, 78, 121
performance, 157, 159

personal planning, 94
personal success, 116–118
personal values, 59–60
personal vision, 57–58
physical legacy, 173, 180
planning: importance of, 73–74;
    personal, 94; significance,
    69–79
profit-sharing plan, 160

Redfern, Rod, 51
repeating of mistakes, 74–75
resiliency: benefits of, 129–130;
    building of, 127; in children,
    141–143; definition of, 123;
    description of, 46–47; example
    of, 124–125; humor and,
    133–134; importance of, 143;
    mental toughness and, 125–130,
    144; nutrition and, 133–134;
    self-talk and, 129; summary of,
    144–145
Right Execution: broader view of,
    162–163; description of, 46;
    focus on, 149; at home,
    163–167; principles of,
    150–161. See also execution
Right Focus: core focus, 64–66;
    description of, 45–46, 69; ele-
    ments of, 49; mission, 50–53;
    purpose of, 49; values. See val-
    ues; vision. See vision
Right Legacy. See legacy
Right People: change in, 100–101;
    description of, 46, 97; home
    team, 111–113; network team,
    109–111; networking for,
    113–116; people classified as,
    46; summary of, 120–121; sup-

port team, 109–111; work team.
    See work team
Right Planning: balanced and
    focused plan, 71–72; descrip-
    tion of, 69; financial planning
    as part of, 86–92; scenario
    learning, 79–86, 141; Signifi-
    cance Plan for. See Signifi-
    cance Plan
robots, 171
Roddick, Anita, 177

scenario creation, 83–85
scenario learning, 79–86, 141
scenario projections, 94
self-awareness, 104
self-reflection, 76
self-talk, 129
Selye, Hans, 126
Senge, Peter, 134, 177
significance: definition of, 1;
    example of, 2–7, 72; life bal-
    ance and, 89–90, 94; position-
    ing of company for, 186; self-
    assessment of, 93; success and,
    173
Significance Plan: balanced and
    focused, 71–72, 75–76; descrip-
    tion of, 69–70; at home,
    165–167; mental roadblocks to,
    77–79
significance planning, 69–79
significance thinking, 173
sinister legacy, 174
social legacy, 180
social network, 116–117, 137
spiritual legacy, 173–174, 181
sports psychology, 125–126
stress: inevitability of, 127; regula-

tion of, 127; response stages of, 126

support team, 109–111

systems thinking, 135–136

Teasley, Harry, 151–152

therapist, 78–79

third-party observation, 138–139

Treat, Gary, 161

trends, 136

value behaviors, 62–63

value themes, 59–60

values: in accountability system, 61–62; conflict in, 61; core, 63–64; definition of, 59; importance of, 64; performance, 62; personal, 59–60; self-assessments, 67–68

vision: attainment of, 132; communicating of, 153; description of, 53; development of, 53–55; mission vs., 53; passions and

values connected with, 175; personal, 57–58; self-assessments, 67–68

"vision litmus test," 56

vision statement: description of, 55; mission statement vs., 58–59

visualization, 131

Wallace, Tom, 108

wellness tune-ups, 113

West, John, 175–176

Wheel of Life, 90–92

Williams, Pam, 91

work team: candidates for, 100–106; description of, 97–98; developmental coaching of, 106–108; developmental needs of, 108; hiring. *See* hiring; loss of, 98; selection of, 99–100; strengths of, 107–108; weaknesses of, 108